THE LAYMAN'S BIBLE COMMENTARY

THE LAYMAN'S BIBLE COMMENTARY
IN TWENTY-FIVE VOLUMES

THE LAYMAN'S
BIBLE COMMENTARY

Balmer H. Kelly, *Editor*

Donald G. Miller *Associate Editors* Arnold B. Rhodes

Dwight M. Chalmers, *Editor, John Knox Press*

VOLUME 16

THE GOSPEL ACCORDING TO
MATTHEW

Suzanne de Dietrich

Translated by Donald G. Miller

JOHN KNOX PRESS

ATLANTA, GEORGIA

© M. E. Bratcher 1961

Published in Great Britain by SCM Press Ltd., London.

Sixth printing 1975

Complete set: ISBN: 0-8042-3026-9
This volume: 0-8042-3016-1
Library of Congress Card Number: 59-10454
Printed in the United States of America

PREFACE

The LAYMAN'S BIBLE COMMENTARY is based on the conviction that the Bible has the Word of good news for the whole world. The Bible is not the property of a special group. It is not even the property and concern of the Church alone. It is given to the Church for its own life but also to bring God's offer of life to all mankind—wherever there are ears to hear and hearts to respond.

It is this point of view which binds the separate parts of the LAYMAN'S BIBLE COMMENTARY into a unity. There are many volumes and many writers, coming from varied backgrounds, as is the case with the Bible itself. But also as with the Bible there is a unity of purpose and of faith. The purpose is to clarify the situations and language of the Bible that it may be more and more fully understood. The faith is that in the Bible there is essentially one Word, one message of salvation, one gospel.

The LAYMAN'S BIBLE COMMENTARY is designed to be a concise, non-technical guide for the layman in personal study of his own Bible. Therefore, no biblical text is printed along with the comment upon it. The commentary will have done its work precisely to the degree in which it moves its readers to take up the Bible for themselves.

The writers have used the Revised Standard Version of the Bible as their basic text. Occasionally they have differed from this translation. Where this is the case they have given their reasons. In the main, no attempt has been made either to justify the wording of the Revised Standard Version or to compare it with other translations.

The objective in this commentary is to provide the most helpful explanation of fundamental matters in simple, up-to-date terms. Exhaustive treatment of subjects has not been undertaken.

In our age knowledge of the Bible is perilously low. At the same time there are signs that many people are longing for help in getting such knowledge. Knowledge of and about the Bible is, of course, not enough. The grace of God and the work of the Holy Spirit are essential to the renewal of life through the Scriptures. It is in the happy confidence that the great hunger for the Word is a sign of God's grace already operating within men, and that the Spirit works most wonderfully where the Word is familiarly known, that this commentary has been written and published.

THE EDITORS AND
THE PUBLISHERS

MATTHEW

INTRODUCTION

"Good News"

"The Gospel according to Matthew"—the simple title tells us immediately that this book is concerned with "good news," for such is the meaning of the Greek word translated "Gospel."

This good news concerns Jesus of Nazareth. The way in which the Apostles understood their task of preaching is admirably summarized in Acts 10:34-43. It was a question of a *testimony*, given by men who had followed Jesus during his earthly ministry and who had seen him again after his resurrection. They had heard his word, they had seen him act. They had recognized in him the Messiah announced by the prophets. The aim of their testimony was to lead men to faith in Jesus, which accounts for the singular accent put on his death, on the necessity of this death, and on the Resurrection. Precisely because the Cross had been a stone of stumbling for the disciples themselves, because it remained "a stumbling-block to Jews and folly to Gentiles," as Paul said (I Cor. 1:23), the Passion occupies a central place in all of the Gospels. From the beginning of Jesus' ministry, the Cross stood on the horizon; one could even say it stood there from his infancy, for both Matthew and Luke give us from the very beginning a presentiment of the opposition of which it will be the climax. And this opposition is not the result of an unfortunate concourse of circumstances. It is because he is the Holy One of God that Jesus was rejected by men. Men could not endure this Presence which judged and condemned them.

But without knowing it men thus accomplished the fixed purpose of God. Everything that happened had been foretold by the Scriptures. In his own Person, Jesus both announces and inaugurates the Kingdom of God. He creates the New Community. He is the Suffering Servant, of whom the Book of Isaiah speaks, who dies, the just for the unjust. He is the conqueror of sin and

death. He is the salvation of the nations. This is the common message of all the Gospels. This is what constitutes the good news,
joyous news.

Distinguishing Features of the Gospel According to Matthew

The Gospel by Matthew was designed for readers of Jewish
origin. In all probability it was written in Palestine, perhaps in
Galilee, or in Syria. This is to be seen in a number of special
characteristics as well as in its general orientation.

1. Jewish customs are familiar to those to whom the Gospel is
addressed. These customs are not given the kind of explanation
that Mark sometimes felt himself obliged to give (compare Mark
7:1-13 with Matt. 15:1-9). Every Jew practiced ritual ablutions. He knew what a phylactery was and why tombs were whitewashed (Matt. 23:5, 27). Matthew is careful to show that Jesus
respected the Law; he only condemned its deformations and
abuses. Jesus wore fringes on his clothing as did all pious Jews
(9:20; compare Num. 15:38). He paid the Temple tax (17:
24-25). He exhorted his disciples to pray that the final catastrophe
would not arrive on the Sabbath (24:20). On the other hand,
since as Son of Man he announced and incarnated in his own
Person the coming Kingdom, he was Lord of the Sabbath (12:8;
see also 9:14-15); in that he was Son of God, he had the right
not to pay the Temple tax (17:24-26).

Jesus insisted on the fact that those who observed the Law
ought to observe it entire, even to its least commandments (5:
17-20); but to the old Law he opposed a higher law, the law of
the Kingdom, which demanded purity of heart and a love which
reflected that of the Father (5:21-48). Thus this Gospel affirms
simultaneously Jesus' respect for the ancient commandments in
that they were given by God, and his divine liberty as the Son who
inaugurated the New Age.

2. The charges of Jesus against the Pharisees involve two
major points:

They add to the commandments of God "the precepts of men,"
and in so doing they are "blind guides, straining out a gnat and
swallowing a camel!" (15:9; 23:24).

They "preach, but do not practice" (23:1-3). The insistence
on putting into practice the word which is heard is one of the

constant themes of this Gospel. For it is precisely this divergence between "saying" and "doing" which is the snare of "pious" people, their real hypocrisy. It was the sense of their own piety as "practicing" Jews (practicing in the ritual sense) which closed the Pharisees against the message of Jesus, against all the prophetic and therefore revolutionary elements of this message. The true disciple is to be known by the fact that he "does" the will of God (6:10; 7:21; 12:49-50; 21:28-31).

3. Matthew makes a constant use of scriptural proofs; this is, one might say, the basis of his apologetics. True, all the Gospels make a similar use of the Scriptures. There is a continuity between the old and the new revelation. But Matthew adorns his Gospel with references which seem sometimes a little forced to the modern reader. It is without doubt necessary to see here a rabbinic practice of that time; but above all one must grasp the intention and the spirit of it: Jesus revived and accomplished in his Person the destiny of the Elect People. He is the promised heir of David and of Abraham. He is the "King of the Jews" to whom the nations, represented by the Magi, render homage, and against whom hostile forces arise from the moment of his birth. It is in his royal capacity that he proclaims with a sovereign authority the coming of the Kingdom of God and the laws which govern that Kingdom. It is as King of Israel that he dies on the cross. It is as King and Judge that he will return at the last day "on the clouds of heaven" (24:30; 26:64; see Dan. 7:13-14), and that, since his resurrection, all power has been given to him "in heaven and on earth" (28:18). The Old Testament citations are designed to prove to the reader that everything which happened had been foreseen, that absolutely nothing is left to chance, that the sovereign hand of God is on his Son from the beginning to the end. Jesus is King, but an abased King who has voluntarily taken the form of the Servant. He makes his own the destiny of the Suffering Servant of Isaiah. He has taken on himself our diseases (8:17); he was misunderstood and rejected by his contemporaries; he submitted in silence to accusations and outrages (Isa. 53:7).

According to the ancient prophecies, the great final gathering would commence with Israel and afterwards extend to the Gentiles. Matthew is the only one who cites the words of Jesus which show that during his earthly ministry he expected to devote himself first and exclusively to "the lost sheep of the house of Israel"

(10:5-6; 15:24). It is necessary to understand that this is a question of a priority in time. It is to the Elect People that the call to repentance and faith must first be addressed; it is from their midst that Jesus recruits the disciples who will constitute the nucleus of the new community. To attribute to Matthew any racial exclusivism whatsoever would be completely to distort the picture. His picture is certainly consistent with history. If Jesus was rejected by his own people, it was not without his having done everything he could to rally them; proof of this are his words, "How often would I . . . and you would not!" (23:37), and the severity of his judgment on Bethsaida and Capernaum (11:20-24). If the first mission of the Twelve was reserved for Israel, the mandate to evangelize the Gentiles was explicitly entrusted to them after the Resurrection, as is made clear by a number of passages (8:10-13; 10:18; 22:1-10; 24:14). Here again is fulfilled the prophecy of Isaiah: the Servant will be "a light to the nations" and his salvation will "reach to the end of the earth" (Isa. 49:5-6).

4. Matthew has a distinctive preoccupation which might be called "ecclesiastical." Just as God gave to Moses on Mount Sinai the charter of the Old Covenant—the rule of life which should govern the conduct of the Elect People—so Jesus in the Sermon on the Mount promulgated the charter of the children of the Kingdom. Matthew alone reports the mandate entrusted to Peter for the constitution of the new community (16:17-19). Matthew alone gives the first lineaments of church discipline (18:15-20).

5. At the time when this Gospel was written, the Christian communities were experiencing persecution. Certain passages without doubt reflect this situation. The writer was concerned to fortify the faith of the Christians—to remind them that Jesus had foreseen these struggles and that he had foreseen the apostasy of some, the lukewarmness of others (5:11-12; 10:16-23; 24:9-13). What happened to Israel could happen to them also; they could be rejected in their turn. For this reason the writer reminds them with insistence that "many that are first will be last, and the last first" (19:30; 20:16).

The Structure of the Gospel

The writer of the Gospel has composed his work with singular care. Without doubt the words of Jesus and certain narratives had already been grouped in the sources which he used. But an attentive study shows that there is here a more systematic plan— at least in certain of its parts—than is the case with Mark or Luke. The teaching of Jesus is grouped in some "discourses," of which each has a precise theme, and in most cases the narratives which follow the discourses are a sort of concrete illustration of them.

Certain commentators have thought it possible to divide the Gospel into five "books" which would make this Gospel the "Pentateuch" of the New Testament. The present writer hesitates to go this far. But Matthew in the structure of this Gospel is certainly influenced by the Old Testament. The first chapters (1:1 —4:22) are, in a manner, the "genesis" of the story which unfolds itself before our eyes. There is here a double beginning: first, the birth of Jesus Christ, with his dual origin, both human and divine (chs. 1 and 2); and second, the coming of the forerunner who prepares for Jesus' ministry (ch. 3). Along with the latter goes the story of the beginning of Jesus' own ministry (4:1-22).

Verse 4:23 characterizes in a very general manner the ministry of Jesus. Such phrases are repeatedly found in the Gospel and serve as transitions between the different parts of the story; for example, the words of 4:23 are found again in 9:35. These chapters, 4:23—9:34, show Jesus mighty in words and in deeds: he proclaims the Reign of God, and he concretely manifests this Reign by his healings and his miracles.

Verses 9:35-38 introduce what could be called the second discourse, setting forth the instructions given to the disciples before they were sent out on their first mission (ch. 10).

Verse 11:1 is, again, very general. It serves as a hinge between the second and third discourses, the latter, occasioned by the question of John the Baptist, being centered on the person and work of John (11:2-19), and being followed by declarations of Jesus concerning his own mission (11:20-30). The opposition which this mission incites is illustrated by a series of incidents which conclude with some severe words of Jesus against the Pharisees (ch. 12).

The first verses of chapter 13 introduce a fourth discourse of Jesus, in the form of parables (13:1-52).

The series of stories in 13:53—16:12 has a less definite structure. It follows the plan of the Gospel by Mark and ends with the confession of Peter. This confession, in all the Gospels, marks a turning point in the ministry of Jesus. Beginning from this moment, Jesus announces to his disciples his approaching end and tries to prepare them for it.

Chapter 18 may be considered as a "fifth discourse," addressed to the disciples. It groups a series of counsels concerning the life of the New Community—the future Church.

Chapters 19 and 20 follow once more the plan of Mark, but the parable of the Workers in the Vineyard is inserted. Chapters 21 and 22 tell of the entry into Jerusalem and the discussions which took place in the Temple between Jesus and the Pharisees.

Chapter 23 is a discourse against the Pharisees, the most violent Jesus pronounced. From this moment the rupture between him and them is complete.

Chapters 24 and 25 prepare the disciples for the final events— the end of the world, the return of the Son of Man in power and glory. They deal with the final accomplishment of the mission of the Son of God on the earth, the ultimate victory of God over all adverse forces. These discourses are at the same time both warning and promise. The call to "watch" is, as it were, the theme introducing the story of the Passion, which takes up chapters 26 and 27 and ends in chapter 28 with the proclamation of the Resurrection and the mission command of the Risen One to his Apostles.

Authorship and Date

The traditional view, which still has some convinced representatives in our time, is that our Gospel was the work of the Apostle Matthew. This opinion is supported by the testimony of Bishop Papias in the second century: "Matthew set down in writing, in the Hebrew language, some words of the Savior. Each one translated them as he was able."

This view, however, runs up against serious objections. The Gospel is written in good Greek, and the references to the Old Testament follow the Greek translation rather than the original Hebrew. But above all, a close study of the first three Gospels shows that behind our present Gospels are written sources, of which one is our Gospel by Mark—reproduced almost completely by the other two, with some abbreviations and changes of style— and another is some collections of words of Jesus, a part of which are found in both Matthew and Luke. It is difficult to believe that an Apostle would thus make use of a Gospel like that of Mark, which is the work of a disciple, not an Apostle, instead of giving his own personal recollections. On the other hand, Matthew himself may have been the originator of one of the collections of the "words of Jesus" which had already circulated orally in the Church. His Gospel gives special importance to the teaching of Jesus, as was seen in the study of its structure.

It was without doubt after the great persecutions by Nero and the martyrdoms of Peter and Paul that the necessity of writing down the most complete testimonies of the words and deeds of Jesus impressed itself upon the survivors of the first Christian generation. If, as is quite generally admitted, the Gospel by Mark was written between A.D. 65 and 70, Matthew would have been written a little later, between A.D. 70 and 80. There can never be absolute certainty about these questions. But is this really cause for regret?

The biblical writers never attached much importance to the person of the authors. It was the Church which, later, insisted on the apostolic origin of the writings of the New Testament. In reality, the Gospels, even as the other writings of the New Testament, worked their way into the faith of the Church not because of their authors but by their content. The Church nourished herself on their teachings; she recognized in them a "word of God," a testimony inspired by the Holy Spirit. The Gospels express the faith of the Church, which she announced and preached forty or fifty years after the events relating to her Lord—his life, his death, his resurrection. They tell us everything which we, in our turn, should believe—that Jesus of Nazareth, crucified under Pontius Pilate, is indeed the Son of God, the King of Israel, and the Savior of the world. It must always be remembered that in reading the Gospels there is a testimony to faith which can only be received in faith. Only he who takes seriously the promises of God and obeys his commandments will know who Jesus is and, walking beside him on the roads of Galilee, will come to the time when he can say with Peter—not merely by hearsay, not because such is the tradition, but with personal certitude—"You are the Christ, the Son of the living God" (16:16).

OUTLINE

COMMENTARY

THE BEGINNINGS

Matthew 1:1—4:22

One question would naturally arise for the Jewish readers to whom this Gospel was addressed: Who is Jesus? Whose son is he?

Before approaching the ministry of Jesus, Matthew first makes answer to this preliminary question. He sets out to demonstrate, on the basis of the Old Testament, that Jesus is indeed the legitimate heir of David and of Abraham. He shows that God himself has prepared his coming and guided his history from the very first moment, as he had guided the history of his people across the centuries.

Birth and Infancy of Jesus Christ (1:1—2:23)

Genealogy of Jesus Christ (1:1-17)

The modern reader is not much interested in the genealogies which adorn the Old Testament. He willingly passes them by without stopping. The Jews, however, jealously preserved their family records. They were the proof that they belonged to the Elect People. The genealogies which are found in the Bible have a theological significance: they underline the continuity of the purpose of God through history. The genealogy of Jesus announces the fact that the One with whom this book is concerned is the heir of all the promises made to the fathers; in other words, he is indeed the promised Messiah.

The simple designation "Jesus Christ" is in itself a confession of faith: Jesus (Joshua) signifies "the LORD is salvation." "Christ" is the translation of the Hebrew word for "Messiah," which means "Anointed One." The ancient kings of Israel were consecrated by an anointing with oil.

Each of these words has a history. The first, "Joshua," was the name of the man chosen by God to lead Israel to the Promised Land. He was a sign of the "Savior" to come, as the Promised Land was a material sign of the Kingdom of God (see Heb. chs. 3 and 4). This time it is no longer a question of snatching

Israel from the slavery in Egypt, but of saving Israel from her sins (1:21). The term "Christ" gathered up all the Messianic hopes of the Old Testament. The prophets had announced the glorious coming of the "Son of David," and of a kingdom which would have no end, bringing peace and justice on the earth (II Sam. 7:12-13; Isa. 2:1-5; Jer. 23:5-6). The term "Christ," then, means nothing less than the coming of the promised King.

The words, "The book of the genealogy of . . ." (1:1), reproduce literally (in Greek) the words of Genesis 5:1. Here is a new "genesis," a new beginning. The evangelist divides the history of the People of God into three periods. The number 14 (2 × 7) is the symbol of plenitude, of something complete. The first period goes from the call of Abraham to the apogee of royalty under David; the second extends from the beginning of the kingship to the abasement and humiliation of the Babylonian Exile; the third moves from the return from exile to the birth of Jesus, a period during which a faithful remnant maintained and transmitted the faith of the fathers. Thus the plan of God sovereignly unfolds from epoch to epoch up to the hour of its fulfillment.

Some women are mentioned in the course of this long enumeration, and they are not those whom one would expect, such as Sarah, Rebecca, Rachel; but Tamar (Gen. ch. 38), Rahab (Joshua 2:1-24; 6:22-25), Ruth (the Book of Ruth), Bathsheba, the wife of Uriah (II Sam. 11:1—12:25). What has motivated the inclusion of these? Each of these women either had kept the Covenant or had entered into the Covenant by an act of faith. But their names remind us also that the Covenant is a Covenant of grace. This long line of ancestors is not a line of moral saints but of forgiven sinners, through whom the faithfulness of God is ever and again manifested anew. It is certainly intentionally that Matthew mentions Rahab the prostitute, and Ruth the Moabitess. In opening the Kingdom to prostitutes and pagans, Jesus could declare himself the bearer of the divine initiative to which the Old Testament testifies.

In conformity with Jewish custom, Matthew does not give the genealogy of the mother but that of the father, even though Joseph was father only by adoption. In Jewish law, adoption conferred the same status as biological kinship.

Birth of Jesus Christ (1:18-25)

We stand here before the mystery of the Incarnation. To say

that Jesus Christ was conceived by the Holy Spirit and born of the Virgin Mary is at the very least to affirm his double sonship—divine and human.

While the Gospel by Luke centers on the annunciation to Mary and on the humble faith and submission of the Virgin, Matthew's story is centered on Joseph, for it is through him that the kinship to David was passed. The fact that Jesus had been conceived by the Holy Spirit before Mary had known her betrothed exposed her to the suspicion of adultery. Joseph, we are told, was a "just" man, that is to say, upright and good. He wishes neither to excuse nor to reproach the one who has betrayed him. He determines to break off with her secretly. An angel of the Lord reveals the truth to him in a dream. The evangelist thus underscores the fact that it is on a direct order from God that Joseph accepts Jesus as his legitimate son, thus recognizing him as belonging to the Davidic succession. It is noteworthy that this succession never seems to have been contested (see Mark 10:47-48; Rom. 1:3).

It was the prerogative of the father to name a child. In the biblical tradition, a name defines or characterizes a person. In prescribing the name of Jesus, God revealed his mission: "He will save his people from their sins" (1:21). Thus the redemptive role of the Messiah is affirmed from the very first. He will save his people, not from Roman domination, as many hoped, but "from their sins." In him is granted the hope of the centuries: God himself descends among men and comes to dwell on the earth. Jesus is "Emmanu-el," "God with us" (1:23). Whatever may have been the immediate historic meaning of the prophecy of Isaiah (Isa. 7:14), Matthew sees in the birth of Jesus its true accomplishment.

This first chapter of the Gospel is already a complete profession of faith: Jesus, Son of David, Son of Abraham, Son of God, is the promised Messiah, the Savior, "God with us."

The Adoration of the Magi (2:1-12)

The prophecies of the Old Testament do not limit the mission of the Savior to the Jewish people alone. He will be "a light to the nations" (Isa. 42:6; 49:6). "Kings shall see and arise; princes, and they shall prostrate themselves" (Isa. 49:7). The story of the adoration of the Wise Men from the East has therefore a symbolic meaning. A day will come when the East and the West will bow before the King of the Jews who is today ignored and forgotten, and they will "bring their glory" to him (see Rev. 21:24-26).

Thus, right from the beginning, after having underlined the fact that the mission of Jesus was first to his own people (1:21), the evangelist indicates the universal character of his salvation. And astrology is the means which God used to conduct the Wise Men to the crib of Jesus! Their offering and their adoration are, as it were, the announcement that one day all the treasures of the Orient will be laid at the feet of the King of kings. They are also a reminder that the essence of all Christian worship is adoration and offering—offering of ourselves and of our most precious possessions.

In the ancient liturgies of the Church, this first "manifestation" of the glory of the Christ was celebrated on a special day, the feast of Epiphany (the 6th of January).

The episode relating to King Herod shows Jesus as the object of the hostility of the powers of this world from his very birth. But the hand of God was on the infant Jesus as it was ever on the infant Moses. The purpose of God is accomplished in spite of men. God thwarts the plans of the enemy (see Exod. 2:1-10).

The fact that Jesus was born at Bethlehem is the occasion for the evangelist to recall the prophecy of Micah (Micah 5:2). Everything takes place as had been anticipated. Addressing himself to the Jews, Matthew makes scriptural evidence the cornerstone of his testimony. We are less sensitive today to this type of argument. Nevertheless, it is very important to remember that for the entire Apostolic Church the relation of the old revelation to the new was the relation of promise to fulfillment. That is why the New Testament and the Old form an inseparable whole.

The Flight Into Egypt (2:13-23)

The hostility of Herod has not subsided. Usurper of the Jewish throne, he dreads even the shadow of a rival, and his fear draws back from no cruelty.

Dreams play a large role in the story of Joseph as in that of the patriarch Joseph. God warns Joseph of the danger which pursues the child, and Joseph once more obeys without hesitating: he leaves for Egypt.

Egypt, many a time in the history of Israel, had been a land of refuge. Abraham, and later Jacob and his sons, descended there in time of famine. Others had fled there from persecution (I Kings 12:2). At the same time, however, Egypt was a land of exile and slavery, and the reminder of a miraculous deliverance. Jesus is here shown, after a fashion, recapitulating in his own life the experience of his people. He also, from his earliest infancy, knows flight across the desert and is exiled until the all-powerful hand of God leads him back "to the land of Israel" (2: 21). This is what permits the evangelist to apply to him the words of Hosea: "Out of Egypt have I called my son" (2:15; see Hosea 11:1).

Did God truly allow so many innocent children to be massacred? (vss. 16-18). This question immediately poses itself to modern minds. Matthew does not raise it. He knows that the history of the People of God is all strewn with blood and tears. The prophets also recognized this. The rage of man is unfurled upon the Elect of God. Once again in history, the mothers in Israel weep for their children and refuse to be comforted (see Jer. 31:15). Our own time has seen massacres equally shameless. The testimony of the evangelist is that God nonetheless pursues his purpose of salvation.

Herod is dead. He has divided his kingdom among his three sons, giving Judea and Samaria to Archelaus. Archelaus will be hated on account of his exactions, and will be dismissed by Rome in the year A.D. 6 and replaced by a Roman procurator. Herod Antipas inherits Galilee and Perea. He will be met again in the Gospel story. Finally, Philip, a peaceful man, inherits the territory situated to the northeast of Lake Tiberias. It is to this region that Jesus will occasionally retire.

A double dream reveals to Joseph that he should return to Palestine, but should settle in Nazareth. That is why, Matthew infers, Jesus will be called "a Nazarene" (2:23). This statement, which claims to rest on a prophecy, has intrigued interpreters in every age without any positive solution being discovered, since the allusion is obscure. The term "Nazarene" is never used in the Old Testament. Some (Calvin, for example) see in this word a derivation from a Hebrew word of similar sound meaning "to separate," "to consecrate." Other interpreters think of another similar word meaning "a shoot" (Isa. 11:1). According to this view, on the apparently dead stump of Jesse a shoot has sprouted which carries in it the future of the world.

Matthew reacted, no doubt, against the fact that the Nazareth

origin of Jesus was a cause of contempt. Perhaps also the dis-
ciples of Jesus were sometimes confused with the sect of the
Nazirites (see Num. 6). The Gospel underlines the fact that
Jesus' rearing at Nazareth corresponded to a fixed purpose of
God (Matt. 26:71-73; see also Luke 18:37; Acts 24:5).

The major impression carried away from these stories of Jesus'
infancy is of the hand of God on all the events surrounding it.
Striking also is the obscurity in which Jesus lives, for he will
be met with again only at the threshold of his public ministry,
about thirty years later.

John the Baptist and the Baptism of Jesus (3:1-17)

John the Baptist (3:1-12)

The Gospel passes without transition from the infancy of Jesus
to another "beginning": the sudden appearance of the messenger
who prepared for the coming of the Savior. Our translations
somewhat weaken the abrupt character of this entering into a
new subject. John the Baptist speaks with the authority of the
ancient prophets whose voice had been silent for centuries. He
announces the Day of the Lord, the end of the age, the inbreak-
ing of the Kingdom which will be both grace and judgment. For
John the Baptist, as for the former prophets of repentance, the
Day of the Lord is great and dreadful (see Amos 5:18-20; Mal.
4:1-6). To prepare for it, nothing less would do than a radical
change, a conversion of the heart.

But for those who repent and believe, this news is great and
good news. This is what the quotation from Isaiah indicates. Indeed, the passage announces the coming of the King who comes
to comfort his people and to deliver them from their sins (Isa.
40:1-5). John, the writer tells us, is the voice of the herald who
opens the way for the King—nothing more, nothing less. The
dress of John, as his message, called to mind the figure of the
prophet Elijah, about whom there was a tradition that he would
precede the Messiah (Mal. 4:5; see Matt. 17:10-13).

The people came to John from Jerusalem and all Judea to be
baptized. Baptism was no new thing for the Jews. They practiced
ritual ablutions. They probably baptized pagan converts, the
baptism symbolizing that the old man was "drowned" along with
his sin, and born to a new life. But John demanded this mark of
radical repentance of all. And it was to be accompanied by the

confession of sins. This obliged men to see themselves as they
were before God and to acknowledge their faults, the acknowl-
edgment being in itself a deliverance (see Ps. 32:1-5).

People flocked to this powerful preacher. But he was without
any illusions about his success, for he read their hearts. Certainly
there were among those who came to him sincere men who were
weighed down by their sin and whose repentance was genuine.
Jesus later recruited from among them his first disciples (John
1:35-42). But when the Pharisees and the Sadducees came in
great numbers, the anger of the Baptist suddenly exploded. He
labeled them a "brood of vipers." Why this severe judgment?
Who are these men? Since they will be met again and again
throughout the Gospel it is worth while to stop here for an answer.

"Pharisee" means "separate one." At a time when many of the
Jews were neglecting the Law, the Pharisees had separated themselves from the others in order to remain faithful to the commandments of God. There was, then, at the origin of Pharisaism
a very positive determination to obey the Lord. The Pharisees
observed the Sabbath with extreme strictness. They carefully ab-
stained from all impure contact. They multiplied rules, ever
more complicated, which they considered necessary to salvation.
They were, in other words, very pious laymen. But there happened to them what happens so often to sects in every age—they
came to believe that they were the only guardians of the truth,
the only "righteous" ones. They looked upon others from the
height of their own piety, but Jesus reproached them for having
passed by the greatest commandment: love. This is not to say
that there were not among them some men of sincere piety. Although John the Baptist, and later Jesus, spoke to them severely,
it was because their lives belied their teaching, and that having
received much they were more responsible than others.

The case of the Sadducees was different. To them was entrusted
the keeping of the Temple at Jerusalem and ecclesiastical govern-
ment. The origin of the name "Sadducees" likely goes back to
Zadok, a priest in the time of David. In order to keep their
priestly privileges, the Sadducees were forced to conciliate the
Roman authorities. They were, above all, "politicians," anxious
over their prestige.

In the eyes of John, the gesture made by these men coming to
be baptized by him was only a sham repentance. As serpents
leave their holes and flee at the approach of fire, so these men

believed that they could by this gesture escape the coming judgment. This achieved nothing. True repentance is recognized by its
fruits. They were not children of Abraham but children of the
Devil (see a similar judgment of Jesus in John 8:44). It is not
sufficient to have glorious ancestors: "God is able from these
stones to raise up children to Abraham." The tree of Israel has
many a time been pruned. This time the ax blows would be laid
at the very root. Everything that does not bear fruit will be cast
into the fire (see Matt. 7:18-19). This is a grave warning, which,
through Israel, is addressed to "religious" men of all times, putting
us all on our guard against our facile religiosity, our self-righteousness, our false securities.

John knows himself to be, and wishes to be, only a forerunner.
He can only call to repentance. He is not even worthy to render
to the One coming after him the ordinary service of a slave; he
is not worthy to carry his sandals. In veiled terms, John thus
announces the arrival of the Messiah whose baptism will be
with the Spirit and with fire (vs. 11; Mal. 3:1-3; Isa. 11:1-5). He
alone is qualified to beat out the grain on his threshing floor and
separate the wheat from the chaff.

The justice and the holiness of God are a consuming fire
which destroys and purifies: ". . . who can endure the day of his
coming . . . ?" (Mal. 3:2). Only those who have recognized the
gravity of this will understand why the gospel of Jesus is "good
news," the way of salvation.

The Baptism of Jesus (3:13-17)

The translation of verse 13 does not reflect the present tense
of the word "come" which seems to be used to underline the un-
expectedness of this event. Matthew is the only one of the evangelists who notes John's disturbance over Jesus' coming. This man
of God discerns in the one who comes to him, if not the Messiah
(see Matt. 11:3), at least one before whom he, John, is an unworthy sinner. John was not the only one to be astonished by
this. Indeed, Christians in all times have posed the question: If
Jesus is without sin, as the New Testament affirms (Heb. 4:15;
I Peter 2:22; II Cor. 5:21; I John 3:5), why did he request baptism for the remission of sins?

The response of Jesus is enigmatic: ". . . it is fitting for us to
fulfil all righteousness [or all that which is righteous]." The righteousness of God, in the Old Testament, is his fidelity to the Cove-

nant which he had made with his people. It was his holy will to
maintain or to re-establish right relations between him and his
people. Here it is simply indicated that Jesus' baptism was willed
by God and conformed to his order. It is only later that the profound meaning of this act may be grasped—that by this act Jesus
identified himself with his people, took on himself their guilt, and
received with and for them the baptism of repentance. The Messianic meaning of this act is to be seen from the rest of the story.

The heavens opened at the moment when Jesus came up out
of the water. The Spirit descended on him in the form of a dove.
The significance of the dove is not very clear. Is it a symbol of
purity? Or of divine life?

God himself makes his voice heard, proclaiming that the one
baptized with water and with the Spirit is his beloved Son. This
word calls to mind both Psalm 2:7 and Isaiah 42:1-4; that is, it
brings together the King-Messiah and the Suffering Servant. God
glorifies his Son in the very moment when he, in self-humiliation,
makes the shame of humanity his own. It is significant that this
voice is heard a second time in the course of Jesus' ministry,
and that it happens at the scene of the Transfiguration, which
immediately follows the announcement of his suffering (Matt.
17:5). Thus are revealed at one and the same time the Messianic
character of the mission of Jesus and the form which his vocation
will take—not that of a glorious Messiah, but that of the suffering
and humiliated Servant. It is this Servant whom God "glorifies"
at the very moment of his humiliation by declaring him his beloved Son.

The Temptation and the Beginning of Jesus' Ministry
(4:1-22)

The Temptation of Jesus (4:1-11)

It is the Spirit who leads Jesus into the wilderness "to be
tempted by the devil." At first sight this appears strange: God
exposing his Son to the blows of Satan. But is it not to battle the
one whom John calls "the prince of this world" that the Son came
to earth? The struggle of Jesus cannot be fully understood if we
do not believe, with the Bible, in the objective reality of an evil
power at work in the world, a power which from the first hour up
to the very end seeks to defeat God.

The temptation of Jesus is closely related to his Messianic vocation. It is also a reminder of the history of the Elect People. We have seen the infant Jesus symbolically reliving the Exodus of his fathers. He now experiences their testing in the wilderness. Moses fasted "forty days" on Sinai when God revealed his will to him (Exod. 34:28). Israel spent forty years in the wilderness (Deut. 8:2). Elijah traveled forty days toward the "mount of God" (I Kings 19:8). This figure, therefore, has a symbolic significance: it designates both the time of testing and the time of revelation. It is significant that the replies of Jesus are all borrowed from Deuteronomy (8:3; 6:16; 6:13). As God had tested Moses, as he had tested Israel, his first-born son (see Hosea 11:1), so now he tests his beloved Son.

According to Jewish tradition, the Messianic Age would reproduce, and at the same time surpass, the miracles of the time of Moses. The miracle of the manna held a large place in the popular imagination (Exod. 16; John 6:30-31). There was a tradition that the Messiah would appear at the Temple and proclaim liberty to the people (see Mal. 3:1-2). Finally, tradition likewise held that Messiah's coming would open the era of a temporal sovereignty of Israel over the nations.

It is in the context of such hopes as these that the expression "If you are the Son of God . . ." must be understood. Satan was saying: "Will God permit you, his Son, to suffer hunger? Has not all power been given to you? How will men believe on you if you do not show them the signs from heaven which are supposed to signal your coming? Do you not know that this world belongs to me and that I do with it what I will? Without compromise with me you know well that all your efforts are doomed to failure!" A strangely familiar voice!

Jesus did not enter into the game with the adversary. He did not discuss with him. (Was that not the primary fault of Eve?) Jesus opposed him with the all-powerful weapon of the Word of God. There is here a basic lesson for us: Jesus was so nourished by this Word that in the hour of temptation it sprang naturally to his lips. How much more necessary this is for us! To every "If you . . . ," Jesus replied, "*God* says."

The first temptation shows Jesus preyed upon by hunger, that elemental and terrible need of every human being. He truly embraced our condition. He knew hunger and poverty. He was the Son of Man who had "nowhere to lay his head" (Luke 9:58). He refused to save himself, and later he submitted to the mock-

ery of those who watched him die (Matt. 27:39-44). His total
commitment into the hands of his Father will be considered only
weakness, impotence, and defeat in the eyes of the world. But in
this way he became the authentic brother of all the famished, of
all the rejected of the world. It is because he has been made one
of them, because he has completely assumed their sin and their
misery, that he will be all-powerful to deliver them (see 8:17).
Thus truly will he one day be able to say that nourishment given
or refused to a hungry person is given or refused to him (25:
31-46).

Jesus knows that God keeps him, but not in the manner intended by Satan. The second temptation reminds us that Scripture,
depending on how one uses it, may be either the instrument of
God or the instrument of Satan. This also is a warning to us. To
try to force God to reveal himself by some spectacular act is not
the language of faith but of unbelief and impatience (see Deut.
6:16; also Exod. 17:1-7). This is to "tempt God." When the
Pharisees later demand signs from Jesus, signs which would be
proof of his Messiahship, they will be refused (Mark 8:12; see
Matt. 16:1-4). God reveals himself in his own time, and in a
manner which pleases him. The way of the Servant is the way of
simple, plain obedience to the revealed Word. Jesus knows,
through the example of the prophets, that this way will not necessarily lead to success, but more often will lead to suffering and
death.

The last temptation is again a question of a radical submission
to the living God. Jesus refers to the first commandment, the
one which pious Jews recite every day (Deut. 6:13). The enemy
has unmasked himself. The real issue throughout this dialogue
has been a choice between two masters. Jesus' reply is severe:
"Begone, Satan!"

Bread, miracles, power—are not these what false messiahs in
every age offer to the credulity of the crowds? The temptations
summed up in this story will be met by Jesus throughout his
career: when the crowds see in him only a healer (Mark 1:
35-39); when they want to make him king (John 6:14-15); when
his own disciples reject with horror the prediction of the Cross
(Matt. 16:21-23).

This solitary struggle, this initial encounter with the adversary, is as it were the first stage of the ministry which is to
follow. One cannot "enter a strong man's house and plunder his

goods," said Jesus, "unless he first binds the strong man" (12:29).

But there is more here: the story of the temptation gives the counterpart to the fall of the first man (Gen. 3). In contrast to the persistent sin of man who desires to make himself God, is set the attitude of the Son of God who freely chooses the way of service and thus calls into being a new humanity whose purpose will no longer be to dominate but to serve (Mark 10:43-45).

The Beginning of the Ministry of Jesus (4:12-22)

The ministry of the forerunner is completed; that of the Messiah begins. Herod has thrown John into prison. The reasons will be given later (14:3-4). Jesus leaves the banks of the Jordan and withdraws to the north of Galilee, to the shores of the Lake of Tiberias. This territory belonged in olden times to the tribes of Zebulun and Naphtali. Invaded and annexed by Assyria at the same time as the entire Kingdom of Israel (the eighth century B.C.), it had been from that time on paganized. It was this Israel, which "sat in darkness" for more than seven centuries, on whom, as the prophecy of Isaiah indicated, the light of the Savior was to arise (Isa. 9:1-2). This quotation, as used by the evangelist, is a confession of Messianic faith: the light of the new world rises on "Galilee of the Gentiles." And this light is none other than Jesus the Messiah.

The King coming in his Kingdom takes up the proclamation of the herald who had preceded him: "Repent, for the kingdom of heaven is at hand" (see 3:2). The difference is not in the message but in the one who proclaims it: the future becomes a present. In the Person of Jesus the Kingdom of God has broken into the world. This is God's "today." When God speaks, no delay is permitted.

This is magnificently attested in the call of the first disciples. At a single word of the Master, they leave everything—their business, their family (see 19:27). They no doubt already knew Jesus (John 1:35-43); but in the eyes of the evangelist this detail is not important, for the whole force of the call resides in the authority of the one who calls.

The figure employed by Jesus is impressive: It is no longer a question of taking fish from the lake, but of drawing men up out of the abyss of sin and death, catching them in the great net of God!

And these simple men obey without discussion. First they are two, then four: "Immediately they left . . . and followed him" (4:20-22). This "immediately" characterizes, for all time, the obedience of faith.

THE PROCLAMATION OF THE KINGDOM IN WORDS AND ACTS

Matthew 4:23—9:35

The Announcement of the New Age (4:23-25)

Verses 23-25 of chapter 4 summarize in a few bold strokes the ministry which is going to be described in the following chapters: it is a proclamation of the New Age in *words* (chs. 5-7) and in *acts* (chs. 8-9). The formula of introduction in 4:23 is found again in 9:35: Jesus teaches, proclaims the good news, and heals.

Any qualified Jewish man attending the worship of a synagogue was permitted to read and comment on a passage of Scripture. He stood up to read and sat down to teach (see 5:1-2; 13:1-2). Jesus conformed to this custom, as did the Apostle Paul later. He went about the country and taught in the synagogues (4:23; 9:35; Luke 4:16-20; see Acts 13:14-16; 14:1). But he taught also in the open air. He preached the good news. The Greek word suggests rather a *proclamation,* such as that of a herald who speaks in the name of the king. And this joyous news is no other than the coming of the Reign of God. And it immediately translates itself into acts; each healing is a sign of this Kingdom which comes—a victory over sickness, sin, and death.

The fame of Jesus, we are told, extends "throughout all Syria." If the editing of the Gospel took place later than the year A.D. 70 (see Introduction), this expression is more easily understood; for beginning from that time, the Roman province of Syria included Palestine. Verse 25 makes clear that the crowds who followed Jesus came not only from Galilee but also from Decapolis on the east of the Lake of Tiberias, from Jerusalem, and from the whole of Judea.

The crowds flocked to this prophet, this rabbi who spoke with "authority" (7:28-29; see Mark 1:22), who not only announced deliverance but delivered (Mark 1:27). Here was indeed, the evangelist tells us, good news; the dawn of the Messianic Age had broken. It is in this sense that the teaching which follows must be understood: it is inseparable from the Person of the one who gives it.

The Charter of the New Age (5:1—7:29)

These chapters are customarily called "The Sermon on the Mount." They rather contain a series of discourses, or fragments of discourses, and some detached words which the evangelist has grouped here. Jesus, the new Moses, promulgates the new law for the children of the Kingdom. He goes up on "the mountain," doubtless one of the hills surrounding the Lake of Tiberias. This indication, even as the structure of chapter 5, which at several points reflects the Decalogue, is an undeniable reminder of the Law of Sinai. The introductory words have a peculiar solemnity. Jesus goes up the mountain, seats himself, opens his mouth, and teaches. His disciples surround him, but this does not exclude the presence of the crowds.

The Beatitudes (5:1-12; see Luke 6:20-26)

A comparison of the parallel texts shows us that in Luke these words are clothed in direct form. They are briefer, more incisive, and the four beatitudes of Luke have their counterpart in the fourfold "woe to you," omitted by Matthew. We are, then, in the presence of two different versions, and it is likely that Luke's is the more primitive. Matthew does not change the meaning but makes it more explicit.

"Blessed [or happy] are the poor in spirit." The term "poor" has a double meaning in the biblical tradition. It means both poverty and humility. The poor in Israel are those who, both literally and figuratively, have nothing and hope only in God. "Poor in spirit" means those who have the spirit of poverty and of humility (see Isa. 57:15).

The saying, ". . . theirs is the kingdom of heaven," is a simple affirmation that the children of the Kingdom are the "poor" who come to God with empty hands. For them the coming of the Messianic Era is truly "good news," the long-awaited deliverance.

The second Beatitude must be understood in a similar sense (vs. 4). It is a reminder of the Messianic promise: "The LORD has anointed me to bring good tidings to the afflicted . . . to comfort all who mourn" (Isa. 61:1-2). An era of joy is opened in this world for all the oppressed and the suffering, because Jesus is here.

The third Beatitude (vs. 5) also expresses a reversal of things. In the world which we know, power belongs to the strong, to the violent. It is they who "succeed." It is they who "possess the earth." But in the Kingdom, the earth will belong to the humble, to the peaceful, to the "children," to those who put their confidence in God, to those who let themselves be despoiled without bitterness and without anger (see Ps. 37:5-11).

The Messianic Era will be a time when righteousness shall reign on a renewed earth (vs. 6). This was the hope and the constant expectation of the prophets. It was at the same time a matter of the righteousness of God, of his fidelity and his truth illuminating and saving men, and of righteousness in human relations. It is this "righteousness" which characterizes the Messianic King (Isa. 11:5; see 42:1-4; Ps. 72:1-15). Blessed, said Jesus, are those who hunger and thirst for this righteousness, for it will be revealed at the Last Day.

The first four Beatitudes describe men who *wait* for the Kingdom of God with the intense nostalgia of those for whom God is their only hope and stay. And Jesus, in his sovereign authority, assigns the Kingdom to them. He speaks in his capacity as King, who has come to inaugurate the Messianic Age. He is the messenger of joy and comfort, the foretold King of righteousness. But he is also the one who has chosen the way of poverty for himself, who will submit to the injustice of men. He is the master who is "gentle and lowly in heart" (11:29; see 21:5). Thus the Church, in reciting the Beatitudes, meditates on the Lord who has both proclaimed and lived them. But at the time when he pronounced them, the meaning of his words was still veiled, as was his Messiahship.

The four Beatitudes that follow have a character somewhat different from the earlier ones. They deal not so much with a want which is to be filled as with an attitude. Here we are speaking deliberately of an *attitude,* not of a virtue.

The first of these (vs. 7) relates to the judgment of God. Before the tribunal of the Most High and the Most Holy, man can hope only for his pity and his pardon. But how can one who does not pardon, who does not exercise mercy toward his neighbor, anticipate the pardon of God? Jesus later repeats this warning several times (6:12, 14-15; 18:21-35; see also James 2:13). It is God's nature to be merciful. Consequently, he who exercises mercy is blessed; he thereby shows himself to be a son of his Father in heaven (Luke 6:35-36). He bears the stamp of his Father.

Purity of heart (vs. 8) is essentially "integrity" or "honesty" of heart, as is set forth in the Psalms (Pss. 24:3-4; 51:10), sincerity of intentions and attitudes, truth, transparency of being— all of which translate themselves into words (5:37) and acts (7: 21-23). Only the one who is "true" in this profound sense can face the judgment. He comes to the light (John 3:20-21), and this light will one day be revealed to him in all its fullness (I Cor. 13:12; I John 3:2).

Verse 9 speaks of "the peacemakers." The word "peace" in the Old Testament expresses health, well-being, harmony, the return to unity of that which has been divided and torn asunder. The longing for peace is so profoundly anchored in the heart of humanity that it has always looked forward to a world where peace would reign among men. In the Bible this hope is often associated with the coming of the Messiah. He is the "Prince of Peace" (Isa. 9:6). A humanity reconciled with God will know peace (Isa. 57:18-19; 60:17). In the New Testament, this reconciliation is the work of Jesus Christ. He is "our peace" (Eph. 2:13-14).

The term "son of God" is applied in the Old Testament to Israel (see Hosea 11:1). Jesus used it on several occasions as applying to the believing individual (see Matt. 5:45-48). God, at the Last Judgment, will recognize as his "sons" those who belong to him (Rev. 21:7; see Rom. 8:13-14, 19, 23).

God is a God of peace. Those who, here below, are the instruments of peace among men, and between God and men, bear the stamp of their Father.

The next Beatitude (vs. 10) deals once more with demeanor or attitude. The righteousness of God is to be seen in his faithfulness to the Covenant which he has made with his people. The "righteousness" of the believer is to be seen in his fidelity to God, in his obedience unto death, in his willingness to do battle with unrighteousness in all of its forms. By such fidelity he exposes himself to the misunderstanding and the persecution of men. The Old Testament had already testified to the fact that the destiny of the "righteous" is to suffer, and the figure of the Servant proclaims the One who will redeem the world by his sufferings (Isa. 52:13—53:12).

The first eight Beatitudes form a unity: they must be understood as a Messianic proclamation. Only the One whom God installs as Judge and King of the world can open the Kingdom. And he opens it to the humble, to the "nobodies"; to those who hope only in God; to those who hunger and thirst for "righteousness" and are ready to suffer for it; to those who, having hoped only in the mercy of God, have their hearts open to the pain of others; to the workers of righteousness and peace.

He who spoke in this fashion is himself the incarnation of this righteousness and this love. The teaching of Jesus Christ is inseparable from his Person. It is on his Person that the authority of his word rests. It is because he is present, because in him all the promises of God have been fulfilled, that the Beatitudes are a message of joy. Apart from him, from the righteousness and peace of which he is the guarantor, they could be only our condemnation.

This is likewise true of the ninth Beatitude (vss. 11-12), which is actually a development of the eighth. This development perhaps reflects the experience of the first Christian generation. Persecution is seen as a normal consequence of the vocation of discipleship to Jesus. Blessed is the one who is persecuted because of his fidelity to his Lord—accused unjustly for love of him (the word "falsely" does not exist in all manuscripts, and is perhaps a later addition). He undergoes the lot of the prophets. The Apostolic Church in its preaching frequently came back to this theme of the necessity for suffering on the part of those who do battle for the cause of Christ. To suffer for him, or because of him, is a privilege (Phil. 1:29; 2:17-18; I Peter 1:3-9; 2:20-24; 4:12-14). Jesus himself, on several occasions, prepared his disciples for these struggles (see, for example, the parallel account of this passage in Luke 6:22-23; see also Matt. 10:16-25).

The Beatitudes proclaim a magnificent reversal of our human manner of measuring people and things. It is those whom the world judges "wretched" whom Jesus proclaims blessed. It is those whom the world calls "happy"—the rich, the powerful, those who "succeed," those who know how to gain the esteem of all—of whom Jesus pronounces the final destitution (Luke 6:24-26). One may be "rich" in the eyes of the world, yet poor and empty before God; or "poor" in the eyes of the world, yet rich toward God. The Gospel by Luke expresses this paradox in all its force, while Matthew spiritualizes it (poor "in spirit"), omitting the contrast with the rich. But the profound judgment uttered by Jesus is the same in both Gospels: it is to those who know themselves poor before God, to those who love him with the grateful love of the poor, that he opens the Kingdom.

Salt of the Earth, Light of the World (5:13-16)

The words which Matthew cites here are found partly in Mark 9:50 and Luke 14:34-35 (the salt which loses its savor), and partly in Luke 8:16 (the lamp which is not hidden). The two great expressions, "You are the salt of the earth" and "You are the light of the world," however, along with the picture of the city set on a hill, belong to Matthew's own treasure. It is not by chance that these words are placed immediately after the Beatitudes. Is it not to the children of the Kingdom, to those blessed by the Father, that these words are addressed? Who are "the salt of the earth" and "the light of the world" but they? Here, too, a paradox shines forth: it is these humble believers, these Galilean fishermen who are ignorant of the world and of whom the world is ignorant, these "little ones" who gather around Jesus, on whom the destiny of the world rests! Regal saying! It is not a mere promise, but an affirmation—"You are." From the very moment when the Lord chooses you and calls you, you *are* the salt of the earth and the light of the world.

What is salt? It is at the same time that which gives taste to food and that which prevents its decay. The Law demanded that salt be put on all offerings presented to God, for salt was a sign of "the covenant" (Lev. 2:13). The faith of believers, bearers of the Covenant of God, witnesses to his mercy—is it this salt which makes the world acceptable to God? Or is it this which preserves the world from total corruption and saves it from condemnation? Without doubt it is both. All three Gospels mention the possibility that the salt may lose its "taste" or "saltness." A rabbi of the first century made ironic allusion to this saying, insisting that it is the nature of salt not to lose its taste! The hypothesis, he insisted, is absurd. But Jesus was often deliberately paradoxical. Israel had been, and the disciples of Jesus are, by their calling, insofar as they are witnesses of the truth of God, "the salt of the earth." But if they allow themselves to lose the treasure confided to them, if the salt becomes insipid, it is "no longer good for anything except to be thrown out and trodden under foot by men." Is not this insipidity of the message of the Church, and of those who are its bearers, a danger in every age? When the

Church dilutes its message, it ends by resembling the world around it; it no longer has any real taste; and its message is "trodden under foot" by passers-by.

Judaism, in the time of Jesus, spoke readily of God as the light of the world, but also applied this term to the Law and to the people of Israel. In so doing, it was in line with the Old Testament, where God is seen as the source of all light and of all life (Gen. 1:3-5; Pss. 36:9; 104:1-2). His word is light (Ps. 119:105). The Servant of God is called "a light to the nations" (Isa. 42:6; 49:6), and the Messianic dawn arises as a light on the whole world. Jerusalem is enlightened by it, and in turn it enlightens the nations (Isa. 60:1-3, 19-20; see Isa. 8:22—9:2). This light of God which enlightens the world is God's truth, his righteousness, his fidelity, his love (see Isa. 42:1-7; Ps. 36:5-10).

These Messianic promises are brought to mind in Matthew 4: 15-16. In the Person of Jesus, the promised light has arisen on the world. He is the light of the world—God made visible to men (see John 1:1-13; 8:12; 9:5; 12:46; II Cor. 4:6). Jesus says to his disciples: *"You* are the light of the world" (Matt. 5:14). The disciples are now, in their turn, the bearers and witnesses of the light which emanates from him (see Phil. 2:15; Eph. 5:8, 14). They cannot keep themselves within his orbit of light without reflecting and radiating it. This light can no more be hidden than can a city set on a hill. The traveler sees it from afar. Likewise, the lamp is lighted in order to give light "to all in the house." Who would dream of putting it "under a bushel"? Its reason for being is to give light to those who surround it.

To be light is to do the work of light, to manifest the light by words and acts. No one can be deceived as to the origin of such works. Those who see them give glory to *the Father who is in heaven.* Purely human works can elicit the praise of men. The works of light direct attention toward the One who is the source of them.

A church which shuts herself in from the needs of the world puts the light of Christ under a bushel. To radiate the light of God—his truth, his love—is the Church's reason for existence. The function of light is to set people and things in their true proportion, to reveal their real nature; it is to spread life, joy, beauty, to warm the world in the fire of the love of God.

Of the Law and of Righteousness (5:17-20)

This passage is both very important and very difficult—important because it indicates the position of Jesus vis-à-vis the revelation of the Old Testament; difficult, because it seems to stick to the letter of the Law and to contradict everything which is told us elsewhere of the attitude of Jesus with regard to the austerity of the Pharisees and of his freedom with respect to men and institutions. It is imperative to study these words one by one.

It is to be noted first of all that in the Hebrew Bible "the law" (Torah) and "the prophets" (5:17) are the two most important parts of Scripture, carrying the greatest authority in matters of faith and practice, the more important of the two being the Torah (the Pentateuch). The Law should be understood as the revelation of the will of God, that is to say, it signifies much more than is meant by the word "law" in the language of today.

The coming of Jesus and the new and striking character of his preaching seem to have raised the hope that since the New Age had sounded, this was the end of the Law and its demands. The Apostle Paul ran afoul of similar misunderstanding. Men concluded from his preaching of Christian liberty that "all things are lawful" (I Cor. 10:23-24; see Gal. 5:13-15). In the history of the Christian Church, there has been an oscillation between a legalistic austerity and a so-called liberty which borders on license.

This passage maintains firmly the demands of the Law. The revelation of God is one. Jesus has not come to do away with the words God has spoken in the past, but to "fulfil" them. To fulfill something is to lead it to its end, to realize it completely.

It was only after his death and resurrection that Jesus' disciples understood in what profound sense he "fulfilled" the Law and the Prophets, and thus fulfilled "all righteousness" (see 3:15). He made himself obedient unto death. To do the will of God was his "food" (John 4:34; see Heb. 10:5-9). He fulfilled the Law by living it. He fulfilled it also by submitting in his own person to the condemnation which the Law brought against a humanity which had transgressed it. At this point in the ministry of Jesus, the full meaning of this passage is still hidden. But in order to understand the words which follow it, it is necessary to read them in the light of their final fulfillment.

Verse 18 is found in a little different form in Luke 16:17: "But it is easier for heaven and earth to pass away, than for one dot of the law to become void." Jesus categorically refused to weaken in the slightest the strictness of the divine demand. If his discussions with the Pharisees are studied carefully, it is plain that he reproached them for not doing themselves what they enjoined upon others (23:3), adding to the Law of God the traditions of men and trampling under foot the greatest commandment of all, that of love (Mark 7:6-13; 3:1-6).

The Law of God as Moses and the prophets have revealed it will abide as long as the present world endures, that is to say, until it is perfectly fulfilled in the Kingdom where all will be righteousness, love, and truth. But in the Person of Jesus this Kingdom had already broken into the world. He is the harbinger of the New Age. For this reason, his word transcends and surpasses that of "the elders." Heaven and earth will pass away, but *his word* will not pass away (24:35).

Obedience to all the commandments of God is once more underscored in verse 19. Nothing is little or negligible when it is a question of the will of God. He who by subtle arguments tries to change the Law, or to diminish its importance, is guilty. One who teaches such casuistry is still more guilty. Jesus seems to say that there are degrees in the Kingdom. Those who have taken the will of God seriously in the smallest things will be "great." Faith does not dispense with obedience; it produces it as the tree bears fruit (see James 2:14-24). And the Apostle Paul says nothing different (Gal. 5:13-26).

There is, nevertheless, a difficulty in this passage which it is necessary to recognize. Did Jesus intend to retain, at least for the Israelites, all the demands of the Mosaic Law? Did he intend these words to be taken literally? It would appear that he so intended. But it is not to be forgotten how Jesus himself summarized the Law (22:34-40). Nor is it to be forgotten that through the Holy Spirit the believer, through faith in the Risen Christ, has indeed passed from the world regulated by law into the world of grace and of love. In emphasizing the strictness of the Law, Jesus shuts us in under the condemnation from which he alone is able to deliver us. Matthew 5 enables us to understand better Paul's shout of deliverance (Rom. 7:24—8:4).

The Pharisees and the scribes were known as scrupulous observers of the Law. They were specialists, if one may so say, in its study and its teaching. Jesus placed on them a severe judgment; if the "righteousness" of the disciples did not surpass theirs, they would not enter into the Kingdom of heaven. It might, therefore, be asked: Who then can enter?

This passage introduces the discourse recorded in 5:21-48, which shows what the higher righteousness is, the law of the Kingdom which Jesus alone can proclaim, because his life is the incarnation of it.

The New Righteousness (5:21-48)

We are here confronted with six antitheses which contrast the "law of the elders" with the new righteousness which Jesus proclaims. "You have heard . . . But *I* say to you." We note first of all the structure of this discourse, which gives it a striking unity. Nevertheless, this unity is broken by some words which refer to the same subject, and which the evangelist has likely for this reason inserted here, but which are found in other contexts in the other Gospels, thus permitting the supposition that they were not a part of the original discourse (compare 5:25-26 with Luke 12:58-59; 5:29-30 with Mark 9:43-47 and Matt. 18:8-9; 5:32 with Luke 16:18; Mark 10:11-12; Matt. 19:9).

Jesus completes and corrects the Law of Moses; in fact, three of the examples given are from the Decalogue (Exod. 20:13-14, 16). Jesus presents himself, then, as the new Moses, who alone can speak with such sovereign authority. It is clear that what he says in no way abrogates the ancient Law. But Jesus goes behind the act to the intention which prompts it, to the secret purposes of the heart. He speaks as the one who is to change hearts of stone into hearts of flesh (see Ezek. 11:19-20), as the one who writes God's Law on men's hearts (Jer. 31:33).

Anger equals murder (5:21-26). The Old Testament condemns murder; it falls under the stroke of penal law. But for Jesus, anger is already murder, for it carries murder in germ. Whoever sins by angry thoughts deserves to be brought before the local magistrate; whoever goes so far as to insult another (see margin: "Raca" means imbecile, empty head!) deserves to appear before the supreme tribunal (the Sanhedrin); and whoever calls another "fool" or "insane" (the Old Testament calls him who denies God a "fool," Ps. 14:1) deserves the fire of judgment, because he thus calls down on his brother a divine curse. This word of Jesus seems hard. It is necessary to catch the irony in it—what court would be sufficient for such a task?—but also to grasp its terrible truth. "Any one who hates his brother is a murderer, and you know that no murderer has eternal life abiding in him" (I John 3:15).

Verses 23-24 introduce us to a feature of Jewish piety: all faithful Jews went up to Jerusalem to present their offerings. Vain gesture, Jesus tells us, if one has offended his brother, for the brother stands between him and God. This is a warning to "religious" people of all times. A right relation to one's brother is one of the conditions which must be fulfilled if God is to accept our worship and our offerings. Verses 25-26 seem at first reading to be a pure counsel of human wisdom: it is dangerous to set the judicial machinery in motion; it ends in ruin! This verse, however, must be understood as a parable. The believer is a man on the way to the courtroom of God; let him be reconciled to his brother while there is still time, in order that his brother may not be his accuser at the Last Judgment.

Lust equals adultery (5:27-32). It is the lustful look, Jesus tells us, which is already an act of adultery. It is committed in the "heart," but it stains the heart as much as the act itself. It is better to lose an eye or a limb than that the whole body should be burned. Lust is one of the temptations which must be overcome by ruthless measures. Salvation demands a radical treatment.

To this word Matthew adds another on divorce which is found elsewhere in another context (19:3-9; see Mark 10:2-12; Luke 16:18). Jewish law permitted a husband to repudiate his wife on condition that he give her "a bill of divorce" (Deut. 24:1-2). This law permitted a new marriage. Jesus listed himself as out of accord with this tolerance which, he said, makes an adulterer of the woman as well as of her second husband.

Only unfaithfulness on the part of the wife can be a proper motive for divorce, for in this case a rupture of the marriage has already taken place (vs. 32). The Gospel by Mark omits this exception and simply sets forth the absoluteness of the divine demand: God has created the unity of the couple and nothing can break it, except "hardness of heart" (Mark 10:2-9). The Mosaic Law makes allowance for this hardness. But the nature of the children of the Kingdom is precisely a changed heart. Here, as in the entire Sermon on the Mount, we are confronted with the absoluteness of the love of God. Marriage is to be understood in the light of the divine purpose, not of human contingencies. For one who takes God seriously, divorce is not a question of "extenuating circumstances" but of a holy will, before which he is obliged to acknowledge himself a transgressor.

Let your Yes be Yes (5:33-37). The Old Testament permits the taking of an oath and has a dreadful severity against false testimony, which in fact consists in taking the name of God in vain (Exod. 20:7, 16; Lev. 19:11-12; Num. 30:2; Deut. 19:16-20). It is a question whether Jesus condemned all oaths, or whether he insisted that every word spoken should have the seriousness of an oath, that is, be spoken before a holy God who reads the heart.

In the Judaism of Jesus' time, it was an established custom to avoid pronouncing the name of God, and to swear instead "by heaven" or "by the earth," or "by Jerusalem," or by one's "head." Jesus rejected these vain subterfuges (see Matt. 23:16-22). Is not God the Master of heaven and of earth, and of the lives of each one of us? (5:36; see Luke 12:7).

A repeated "Yes, Yes" or "No, No" had the value of an oath for the Jews; that is to say, it marked the seriousness of a reply. Jesus himself sometimes prefaced a particularly important declaration with an "Amen," or even with a double "Amen" which is translated "Truly, truly." The "Amen" was like a signature affixed to a declaration (see Deut. 27:15-26; Neh. 5:13; Matt. 5:18; 6:16; 8:10; John 3:3-11; 5:19, 24, 25).

The oath has meaning only in a world where falsehood reigns; that is its reason for existence in judicial matters. The children of the Kingdom, however, know that God hears all their words and that they will have to give account for them to him. They, therefore, do not know how to say both Yes and No at the same time (see II Cor. 1:17-20). Each "Yes" binds them entirely. Anything added to it comes from the Devil, who is "the father of lies" (see John 8:44).

Resist not evil (5:38-42; see Luke 6:29-30). The law of retaliation (Lev. 24:17-20) may seem to us severe. As a matter of fact, however, in its time it was a limitation on the arbitrariness of individual or collective vengeance (see Gen. 4:15-24). The principle that punishment should be in proportion to the crime is the very foundation of all law. In the time of Jesus, the Mosaic Law was no longer applied in its original preciseness. Jesus was, therefore, not protesting against any current abuse, but was rather

dealing with a law regarded as legitimate, calling it into question
in the name of a higher justice—the justice which governs the
sons of the Father who is in heaven (5:45-48; see Luke 6:35-36).

If God dealt with us according to strict justice, what would
become of us? Jesus was certainly not intending to abolish the
Law, the necessity of which he elsewhere acknowledged (5:25;
John 19:11; see Rom. 13:1-5), but was indicating the limits of
Law in the light of the fact that God's love has other norms. It
was a question here of not responding to violence with violence;
of allowing oneself to be insulted (vs. 39) and, if need be,
robbed (vs. 40); to go beyond what is forced upon one (vs. 41).
This last was likely an allusion to forced labor, such as Roman
legionnaires could require of passers-by. To grasp the thought
of Jesus, it is necessary to look at him, who did "not resist"
but consented to every shame (see Isa. 50:5-6; 53:7-8; Matt. 26:
52-53; I Peter 2:19-24). It is to follow on this way—the way of
the Cross—that he invites his own.

Love your enemies (5:43-48). This passage presents a difficulty. The Old Testament never commanded hatred for enemies.
This word, then, must relate rather to an attitude current in Jesus'
day, which the Jews have not been the only ones to practice! For
them, the love of neighbor limited itself to those of their own
people, or those who shared their faith. The frequent expressions
of hatred found in the Old Testament are addressed to the enemies
of God whom the faithful identified (perhaps a little too quickly!)
with their own enemies (see Pss. 139:19-22; 140:9-11). To hatred
Jesus opposes love and prayer for persecutors, for by these ways
men become sons of their Father who is in heaven. This phrase
gives us the key to the whole passage, indeed to the entire discourse: the real question is whether our deportment carries the
mark of our divine sonship, or whether it is only like that of the
"tax collectors" and "Gentiles," that is, those who do not know
the miracle of being loved by God.

"You shall be holy; for I the LORD your God am holy" (Lev.
19:2); this the Old Covenant tells us. "You, therefore, must be
perfect, as your heavenly Father is perfect"; this Jesus tells us.
And Luke is doubtless right in indicating that this "perfection"
consists above all in *mercy* (Luke 6:36).

If in the Sermon on the Mount we have merely a system of
ethics, or of a self-sufficient morality, then its demands must
overwhelm us. It has often and rightly been reproached for lacking

realism, for demanding the impossible. The Sermon on the Mount
is "good news" only if we receive it from the mouth of the One
who himself lived it and who, by his grace, desires to live it again
in us, to transform us into his image, to make us authentic sons
of the Father. Otherwise, it remains for us only a judgment, for
it lays bare all the avowed or hidden refusals of a heart which
is in rebellion against the divine law. But it is also a call and a
promise, a glorious opening on the coming Kingdom of which,
by faith, we are the children.

Of Alms, Prayer, and Fasting (6:1-18)

We have here three strophes of identical structure, all of which
conclude with the same expression: "your Father who sees in secret will reward you." The evangelist has inserted between the
second and third strophes two other words relative to prayer, and
the Lord's Prayer.

These three strophes deal with three forms of Jewish piety.
Here again, Jesus constrasts two conceptions of "righteousness":
a "righteousness" which seeks the approval of men and a righteousness on which the secret blessing of God rests. Each of these
types of righteousness wins the reward which comes from it.
Here, as throughout the Sermon on the Mount, the issue involves
the true situation of man before God—the genuineness of man's
benevolence, his prayer, and his repentance. God "sees in secret."
He unmasks all the hypocritical acts done not out of love but to
be "seen by men." A true encounter with another demands the
forgetting of self, an unostentatious reserve. A true encounter
with God takes place "in secret." A love which displays its favors
or its sacrifices is not love—it is a caricature of love.

What is said here of alms applies to all our works, just as what
is said of fasting applies to all our renunciations. It is better
that God alone know of them. It is preferable that the one who
does them have no consciousness of them, because they spring
forth spontaneously from a renewed heart. The blessing of God
rests on such, and he will receive his reward "at the last day."

Jesus urges his disciples to sobriety in prayer (vs. 7). It is the
pagans, said he, who believe that the longer a prayer, the more
efficacious it is. (Is it only pagans who believe this?) The rever-
ence we owe to God demands that we weigh our words (see Eccl.
5:2). God knows what we have need of before we ask him! (vs.
8). Therefore, someone will object, why pray? The prayer which

Jesus teaches his disciples answers this question. It is less a request than an act of faith and of praise, a giving of our whole selves to God in order that his will may be done in us and by us. This prayer focuses on God, on his Kingdom; it aims at putting our whole being and its desires in tune with God, as one tunes an instrument so that it may give a purer sound.

"Our Father who art in heaven." This formula, peculiar to Matthew (see Luke 11:2), evokes both the intimacy of the filial relation and the majesty of God; it reminds us that "God is in heaven, and you upon earth" (Eccl. 5:2). We wait before a holy God, but a God who, in Jesus Christ, desires to be "our Father." The whole miracle of divine grace is contained in this single word.

"Hallowed be thy name." In Hebrew tradition, the *name* is equivalent to the person; it reveals him. It is said of Israel that she sanctifies the holy name of God by her obedience to his commandments, or profanes it by her disobedience (Lev. 22:31-32; Isa. 29:23; 48:9-11; Ezek. 36:22-27). The sanctification of the name of God is one of the signs of the Messianic Age: God will finally be acknowledged and glorified for what he is, and manifested through his children. The Christian has the weighty honor of bearing the name of Christ. Each day he must face the question of whether his conduct "hallows" this name or desecrates it.

"Thy kingdom come." The hallowing of God's name is intimately related to the coming of his Kingdom. This involves the victory of God over all his enemies, and the coming of the New Age, the new heavens and the new earth where righteousness shall reign (Isa. 65:17-18; see II Peter 3:13; Rev. 11:15; I Cor. 15:24-28). We have the first fruits of this final victory in Jesus Christ, through the Holy Spirit. But we await its glorious manifestation, and this hope remains the ardent prayer of Christians (Rev. 22:20).

"Thy will be done, On earth as it is in heaven." In the Old Testament, the term translated here by "will" means also "good will," "benevolence," and the New Testament readily uses it in this sense (see Luke 2:14, margin; Matt. 11:26). It suggests God's benevolent purpose toward us, as it is revealed in Jesus Christ. Jesus has come to the earth to accomplish the will of God, which is the salvation of all men (see Heb. 10:7-9; John 3:16; 6:38-40; 12:32). This petition, then, does not imply a mere passive resignation. To pray that God's will be done "on earth as it is in heaven" is to pray for God's victory over all adverse forces which

still hold the world in bondage; it is to pray that all shall come
to know God; it is to pray that his will be done in us and by us.
For a Christian who lives under the sign of the cross and the resurrection of Jesus Christ, to pray this prayer is to enter into battle
alongside his Lord so that Christ may reign on the earth as he does
in heaven. It is, very concretely, a question of knowing the will
of God and of doing it (see Rom. 12:2; Col. 1:9-10). But Jesus
himself has shown us that this knowledge is not acquired without
struggle (Matt. 26:38-39).

These first petitions relate to God. Those that follow present
to God the fundamental needs of men: daily bread, the pardon
of faults, and help in temptation.

"Give us this day our daily bread." This petition poses a problem, for the Greek term translated "daily" appears only in this
place in the New Testament (and its parallel in Luke 11:3). The
etymology of this word is uncertain. It may mean "for this day,"
or "for tomorrow," or "necessary." In any case, it involves a mini-
mum of provision indispensable to life. It has sometimes been
spiritualized, as though it meant bread for the soul. But our
bodies also receive the life of God and depend on him for their
existence. It is his entire existence which the believer entrusts
to God, and it is this trustful prayer which ought to deliver him
from fear of the morrow. There is, then, no contradiction between this petition and Jesus' words against anxiety of spirit
(6:25-34).

"And forgive us our debts." God is seen here as the sovereign
creditor to whom we must give account for all the goods he has
entrusted to us. What have we that we have not received? The
pardon which God offers signifies that the past is abolished and
that a man finds himself before God in an entirely new situation.
He is freed from his debt. But if he does not forgive the debts—
infinitesimal by comparison—which his brother has contracted
toward him, his own liberation is illusory. The love of God has
found no echo in him. He is still in death. This is why Jesus
inexorably bound the pardon which we receive from God to that
which we accord to others (see 6:14-15; 18:23-35; Mark 11:25;
see James 2:13).

"And lead us not into temptation." This saying has posed a
problem for Christians in every age. The Epistle of James tells
us that God "tempts no one" (James 1:13-14). The source of
temptation is not in God. It is in our own "desire," or it comes

from "the tempter"—Satan (I Thess. 3:5). We are, nevertheless, told that God "tests" his own (Gen. 22:1; Exod. 16:4; Job 1:6-12). He places us in circumstances which put our fidelity to the test. The New Testament is full of warnings about the struggles which await Christians in the last days (see Matt. 24:4-13; Luke 22:31). Jesus faced temptation and recognized in his struggles the will of God (Matt. 4:1; see John 12:27-31; 14:30-31; Heb. 4:15). He tells us to fear temptation, to watch and pray in order to be preserved from it, precisely because he alone has measured the total force of it (Matt. 26:40-41).

"Deliver us from evil." The Greek term translated "evil" designates in biblical language everything which is wicked or perverse; that is, everything which is opposed to God, to his will, to his law, to his revelation. The noun form may be either neuter, "evil," or masculine, "the evil one," meaning Satan (Matt. 13:19; see Mark 4:15; I John 2:13-14). In Matthew 6:13 both interpretations are possible. This petition is closely bound to the preceding one. It is directed, as is the entire Lord's Prayer, toward the final deliverance, toward the ultimate victory of God over all evil powers. But the one who teaches it has come into the world to announce and inaugurate the Reign of God, to do his will, to give assurance by his sacrifice of the pardon of sins, to conquer in his own Person the tempter of men. Hence, the Lord's Prayer expresses both our *future* hope—"thy kingdom come"—and our *present* hope; for it is from day to day that we need bread, pardon, and divine protection against temptation and the power of evil.

According to the oldest manuscripts, it is at this point that the Lord's Prayer ends. But a doxology was added very early. This was an act of praise which, in all probability, was originally the response of the faithful as the Lord's Prayer was pronounced by one of them. This act of adoration brings to mind I Chronicles 29:11. The One whose glorious manifestation we await in faith is the Almighty who reigns for ever and ever.

The Lord's Prayer ought not to be understood only as a liturgical "formula." Jesus sets forth in it what should be the character of all true prayer. It is, first of all, an act of adoration, an act of faith and hope in the Reign of God, in the New Age of which, in Jesus Christ and through the Holy Spirit, we have the initial installment; then an act of consecration to God's will; and finally, a humble and total commitment of our needs to the Father, in the assurance that he will faithfully supply them.

Of Treasures and the Spirit of Anxiety (6:19-34)

We have here four sayings, or groups of sayings, which are found in Luke in different contexts (Luke 12:33; 11:34-36; 16:13; 12:22-31). They form a unity in that they deal with our attitude with regard to earthly goods.

Verses 19-21 contrast the treasures of this earth, doomed to destruction, with eternal possessions. There is no suggestion of a conception which was current in the time of Jesus, that is, the assurance of a recompense in heaven for our good deeds, such as, for example, the giving of alms. The question here is whether the first loyalty of our hearts is to God or to the things of this world. He who is engrossed in accumulating possessions is in danger of setting his heart on riches and making an idol of them, thereby forgetting eternal realities (see Luke 12:16-21, 33-34).

The parable in verses 22-23 likewise contains a contrast—between a healthy eye which illuminates the whole man and the kind of double vision which makes the whole man "full of darkness." The issue is whether the gaze is open only to God or is closed to his light by trying to look to possessions as well. The heart was conceived as the center of the being. If the heart is set on God, all thoughts and actions are directed toward him and are illuminated by his presence. If the heart is shut against God, or attached elsewhere, all is in obscurity, both within and without.

The parable of the Two Masters (vs. 24) was inspired by the custom of that day which permitted a slave to belong to two masters. This involved inevitable conflict. The origin of the Aramaic word "mammon" is uncertain. It seems to signify "that to which one entrusts himself." Hence, it came to designate money, the capital which one retains (everything one possesses which is negotiable). In Judaism it took on a bad flavor ("unrighteous mammon," Luke 16:9-11). Jesus sees in mammon the personification of riches, a demonic power which holds man under its control. The worship of mammon excludes the worship of God, and vice versa. There is a radical incompatability between the two. If our heart is devoted to one, it cannot but hate the other, for each demands exclusive ownership. No one ever unmasked the power of money and the fascination which it holds for men as did Jesus.

Verses 25-34 are addressed particularly to the "poor" in the sense given to this term in the Beatitudes—those whose expectation and hope are in God, those who have "left everything" to follow Jesus (vs. 33; see 19:27). How will it be with them? Who will ensure them their daily bread? Here is a reassuring word—their destiny is in good hands! The Father who watches over the birds and the flowers, will he not with still greater reason watch over his children?

It would be a distortion of this passage to see in it an encouragement not to work, and to expect everything from God without doing anything (see II Thess. 3:8-12). These words are addressed to those who "seek first his kingdom and his righteousness"; that is, those who have devoted their lives to God. To this total gift of themselves God will respond by giving them what they seek—his Kingdom!—and all other things will be added as well (vs. 33). Jesus did not preach carelessness, but the commitment to God, in humble and joyous faith, of all our cares, particularly the care which wracks so many people—anxiety over the morrow. This anxiety includes, but goes beyond, material cares. It may be fear of old age, fear of death. It is not in our power to add "one cubit" to the span of our lives. We must rather receive life from God day by day, and live under the gaze of our Father to the best of our possibilities, in gratitude for what he gives us, and in the confident certainty of never being abandoned. Anxiety is pagan. In fact, it denies the love, the faithfulness, and the omnipotence of God. It chains us to the things of earth.

But does not anxiety often besiege us in spite of ourselves? True; it does. It is a "temptation" from which God alone can deliver us (see Phil. 4:6-7). But in the last analysis it always springs from our desire for external securities, from our refusal to commit to God alone the care of our life and of our death.

Warnings and Exhortations (7:1-14)

Chapter 7 is made up of detached sayings, the most part of which are found also in Luke, under a form scarcely different but in other contexts.

The logical bond which ties these sayings together is less evident than in the preceding chapters. They are rather a series of exhortations and warnings, leading on to the solemn conclusion of the whole discourse (7:21-27). Only verses 1-5, 15-20, and 24-27 are found in the "discourse" of Luke 6, where they have a stronger cohesion.

The main point of the passage in 7:1-5 resumes that which appeared earlier with regard to mercy (5:7) and pardon (6:12,

14-15). The one who judges—that is, denounces the faults of
others—will be judged, not at the tribunal of men but of God.
To judge others is to substitute one's self for God, who alone is
qualified to weigh the actions of men (see I Cor. 4:3-5). God
will "measure" us as we have "measured" others—with severity
or with charity. The parable of the Speck and the Log, deliberately
paradoxical, illustrates the thought of Jesus—we see the slightest
faults in others, while the most enormous faults of our own escape us. If we knew how to recognize that which blinds us, perhaps we would know how to help others. On the contrary, however, we denounce the faults of others in order to cover our own
tracks from ourselves and from others. This is our hypocrisy.

This passage is not dealing with the exercise of the kind of
judgment whose necessity is recognized by both the Old and the
New Testaments (Deut. 1:16-17; 16:18-20; Rom. 13:1-5); nor is
it dealing with the discipline which should be exercised in the
Church (Matt. 18:15-17). It relates rather to those facile judgments which, without love, we make of one another, and to the
subtle poison of the sins of the tongue (see James 3:1-10).

It is not difficult to see a connection between the saying in verse
6 and the preceding one, even if it were made only in the mind
of the editor. The two sayings are complementary. Jesus condemns
judgment, but he enjoins *discernment*.

Dogs and swine are regarded by the Jews as unclean animals.
It is especially necessary in interpreting this passage to avoid
what is often done—applying these expressions to Gentiles and
tax collectors. This would be wholly contrary to the attitude of
Jesus toward them (see 9:10-13). They would apply at the most
only to those in these groups who deliberately rejected his word.
But it is much better to see an analogy in this double image used
by Jesus. Dogs are incapable of knowing the difference between
"what is holy"—the term seems to designate the meats offered in
sacrifice—and what is not. Swine are not nourished by pearls; they
trample them under foot and turn against you, furious that you
have deceived them. It is the same with "cynical" men, who have
closed themselves against the things of God—they know only
how to desecrate sacred things, and your regard for such things
serves only to provoke raillery and blasphemies. An illustration of
this warning may be seen in the care with which, according to
the Gospel by Mark, Jesus guarded the Messianic secret up to
the very end of his earthly ministry (Mark 1:34, 44; 8:29-30;

Matt. 13:10-11); or again in his silences, which are in reality his heaviest condemnations (Luke 23:8-9; Mark 14:60-61). One does not show his most precious possessions to the trifling. Thus it is with the divine revelation. There is "a time to keep silence, and a time to speak" (Eccl. 3:7).

The Church very early applied this saying to the Eucharist, understanding that it was to be reserved "for the saints." This was an unwarranted narrowing of its meaning. Does it not rather apply to the total treasure of the faith entrusted to us? It is certainly necessary to proclaim this faith, but with the discernment and the unobtrusiveness of love.

The passage on prayer (7:7-11) is placed in the Gospel of Luke following a whole series of teachings on prayer, of which it is the conclusion (Luke 11:5-13). In the Gospel by Matthew it stands as a detached saying. Without doubt all the preceding exhortations drive us to prayer, and this saying on prayer should be viewed in the light of them. We are not told that no matter what petitions men offer, they will be granted. Matthew's entire discourse applies only to the children of the Kingdom, to those who hunger and thirst after righteousness and the mercy of God, to those whose whole hope is in him. *They* may with assurance ask their Father who is in heaven for every need of their lives. If they seek him, they will find him. If they knock on his door, he will respond. This presumes on the part of those who ask, seek, and knock, an intensity and a seriousness of desire (see Luke 11:5-8).

The parable of verses 9-11 compares the paternal love of men to that of God, and emphasizes how much greater the love of God is. For we are "evil," while he is good. Nothing is told us here of what true prayer is, for that has been indicated earlier (6:5-15). On the contrary, the necessity of *asking* in order to receive is here underlined. We are not told that God will necessarily give what we have asked. But he always responds, and everything that he does in us and for us is good.

Verse 12 is once more a detached saying. It returns to the subject of neighborly love, which is the theme of the whole discourse, and formulates what has been called "the Golden Rule." In a negative form ("Do not do . . .") this rule had become almost a proverb, not only in Judaism but also in the general morality of the time. Jesus was enough of a realist to know how limited our love is, and he proposed a criterion of conduct which

is within the reach of all. To the complicated interpretations of
the Law in which the Pharisees and scribes delighted, he opposed
a simple principle which summed up "the law and the prophets,"
and which would suffice to illuminate our motives and regulate
our acts. In so doing, he once more set in its central place the
ancient commandment (Lev. 19:17-18; see Luke 10:25-27).

In the double parable of the "gate" and the "way" (7:13-14;
see Luke 13:23-25), the total stress is placed on the necessity
of choice, on the fact that there are few who "find" the gate and
the way which lead to life. These words are to be read as a warning. The way which leads to destruction is broad and easy. Men
follow it instinctively, almost without thinking. The way to life is
both difficult to find and difficult to follow. It demands vigilance
at every moment.

Jesus does not state precisely what the door is, or what is
the way. In reality, however, he has been discussing it throughout the entire preceding discourse—in the Beatitudes, in the
teaching on the new righteousness, in all the warnings of chapters
6 and 7. Now the question is boldly posed: To whom do we
choose to belong? Whom will we follow? (see 6:24).

In the Gospel by John we discover what underlies all the affir-
mations and promises of the Sermon on the Mount: the door,
the way, is Jesus himself (John 10:1-2, 7-10; 14:4-6). He is the
one in whom all is accomplished, the one who has opened to
us the way of life. But to follow him is to choose the narrow
way, to renounce self (see Matt. 16:24-26). It is to give all as he
has given all.

Here again it is clear that the ethic of the whole discourse is
inseparable from the Person of the one who spoke it, and who
alone can achieve for us and in us both its promises and its demands.

Of the Authenticity of Faith (7:15-29)

The saying about false prophets is peculiar to Matthew (7:15).
That about good and bad fruit (7:16-20) is found also in Luke
6:43-45.

Who are these false prophets? Without doubt all those who
falsify the word of God and proclaim only "visions of their
own minds" (see Jer. 23:16-32). They represent themselves
as belonging to the flock, although their only thought is to
devour and to destroy (see Ezek. 22:27). In this saying Jesus per-

haps refers to certain leaders of Israel who lead their people astray (see ch. 23). But he chiefly warns his disciples ahead of time that the newborn Church will not be guaranteed against intrigue and error any more than Israel was. There will be false brothers (24:10-11, 24; see II Cor. 11:13-15; I John 4:1).

One knows a tree by its fruits and a disciple by his works. We have been reminded throughout these chapters that the heart must be changed. Jesus now implies that if the heart is changed it will show itself. The new heart will reveal itself in words and acts. The authenticity of faith is manifested in the fruits which it bears (see John 15:1-8; Gal. 5:13-15, 22-23).

Verses 21-23 are a dreadful warning: the most orthodox avowals of faith have no value in the eyes of God if they are not translated into concrete obedience to his will. One may with his lips loudly profess his faith in God, and even invoke Jesus as Lord, yet deny him by thoughts, words, and acts. Such an attitude is worse than unbelief, for it is a hypocrisy destructive of all true faith (see ch. 23). Jesus has just explained in a whole series of teachings what the will of the Father is for his children. The fundamental attitude of sons of the Kingdom is humility and love. All their acts bear the mark of the One who inspires them (5:16). It is important to note that those whom Jesus accuses of "saying" and not "doing" have accomplished all sorts of works. They have prophesied, they have cast out demons, they have performed miracles! But in all these they have sought not God's glory but their own. They declare themselves to belong to the Lord, but they do not know him (see Luke 13:25-27). They have not taken seriously his holy will. They are "evildoers."

This passage, as the entire discourse which precedes it, shows how vain it is to oppose "faith" to "works." For all authentic faith translates itself into obedience. Just as the food of Jesus was to do the will of his Father who is in heaven (John 4:34; 6:38), so his disciples have no other reason for existence than the accomplishment of this will (see Matt. 12:50).

In this passage, for the first time we see Jesus explicitly declaring himself King and Judge, that is, affirming his Messianic mission. He is the one who holds the keys of the Kingdom and will judge the actions and secret thoughts of men at the last day (see 25:31-46). No one can escape from the gravity of this judgment, and it will be the more dreadful as we have received the more. This warning is clearly addressed to those who are his disciples.

The parable which follows in verses 24-27 is addressed to all who hear the word of Jesus. This word confronts them with a final decision. Either they take this word seriously and build their lives on it, or they are indifferent to it, only to find it returning against them at the last day (see John 12:47-48). A faith which does not inform our lives, our whole manner of thinking and acting, is only an illusion and a lie. It cannot endure testing. On the contrary, he who builds life on the promises and commandments of God has nothing to fear from the tempests of life.

Jesus here affirms his sovereign authority. To hear him is to hear God. To build life on his word is to build "on the rock." God is called the "Rock" of Israel in the Old Testament (Deut. 32:4; II Sam. 22:2-3; 23:1-5; Ps. 18:1-3, 31-32, 46). It was on the rock of his word, on his faithfulness, that the "house" of Israel was built. In the New Testament, the new "house" of God is the Christian community. Its foundation is Jesus Christ and his word (see Heb. 3:1-6; I Peter 2:4-8; I Cor. 3:10-11).

These warnings were aimed not only at the people of the Old Covenant. They were addressed also to the new community which was then in process of being created. To believe on Jesus Christ is to practice his commandments (see John 15:12-14).

Thus is completed the teaching to which tradition has given the title "The Sermon on the Mount." The crowds, the Gospel tells us, were struck by his doctrine, "for he taught them as one who had authority, and not as their scribes" (vs. 29). The scribe could only recite and comment on Scripture; but here was a greater than Moses, whose word was clothed with all the authority of God. Jesus himself incarnates the new righteousness which he demands of men. And he alone can communicate it to his own.

Let us repeat once more: to turn this discourse into an ethical teaching detached from the Person of the Savior is to make of it an irremediable condemnation. On the other hand, it would be contrary to all the teachings of Jesus to see in it only an ideal, good for an otherworldly Kingdom of heaven or reserved for a few extraordinary vocations. Jesus intends to be obeyed. To believe on him is to be willing constantly to be judged and called to order by his word. It is to be born into a life of love which he alone can create in us. It is to live from day to day in the pardon of God. It is to exercise mercy toward others, evil as we are, but saved solely by his grace. It is to take his commandments with utmost seriousness.

The Kingdom of God Manifested in Acts (8:1—9:35)

The evangelist has shown us how the unique authority of Jesus
was manifested in his teaching. He now goes on to show how this
same authority was manifested in his deeds. By a series of healings, Jesus reveals himself as the Lord of life and of death. Each
healing is a sign of the coming Kingdom which, in Jesus, is already present.

The Healing of the Leper (8:1-4)

This healing is recorded also by both Mark (1:40-45) and Luke
(5:12-16). Matthew places it immediately after the Sermon on the
Mount. He doubtless sees in this episode a concrete illustration
of the attitude of Jesus toward the Mosaic Law, which has just
been the theme of his teaching.

Leprosy was dreaded as a contagious disease; it also rendered
ritually impure those who were struck by it and condemned them
to flee the society of their fellow men. It was considered to be an
incurable disease. Nevertheless, when the leper was "whitened"
—that is to say, when his flesh was entirely dead—he ceased to
be contagious and the interdict could be lifted by the priest, who
fulfilled the rites of purification (Lev. 13; 14:1-7; see II Kings 5
and II Chron. 26:16-21).

The leper's act of throwing himself at the feet of Jesus is a de-
fiance of the Law. He recognized in Jesus a power which belonged only to God. Jesus, "moved with pity" as Mark tells us,
touched him and said: "I will; be clean." There was more at stake
than the written Law. It was the life and the salvation of a man.
Jesus is thus revealed as master of the Law and as above all "defilement." On the other hand, he shows his respect for the Law
in sending the healed man to the priest and in commanding him
to fulfill all that Moses had prescribed, "for a proof to the people."
The purpose of this may have been to enable them to see that the
power of God was at work in what Jesus had done; or it may
have been to show them the respect which Jesus had for the authority of the priests in their own domain.

The Faith of a Gentile (8:5-13)

The second act of faith related by Matthew (see Luke 7:1-10)
is that of a Roman officer. This man had heard reports of Jesus

as a great healer, so he came to beg him to heal his servant (the word is "young man"). Jesus declared himself ready to go to the house of this man, who was evidently a "Gentile." But the centurion felt himself unworthy to receive Jesus into his home and made an astonishing reply. With the logic of a soldier who knows what it is to obey and to command, he recognized in Jesus an authentic authority which came to him from the highest source— from God himself. Jesus is master of sickness and master of spirits, as he—the centurion—is of his soldiers. A word is sufficient for them to obey him! Jesus marveled. The faith of this man surpassed anything that he had met with "in Israel," that is, among the people of the Covenant and of the promises!

The story, placed here at the beginning of Jesus' ministry, is an announcement of the response which the gospel will one day find among the Gentiles. It is a warning to the "children of Abraham." This thought is developed in the verses that follow (vss. 11-12; see Luke 13:28-30). The Gentiles will come from the east and the west to be seated at the banquet of the Kingdom, while those who believe themselves to be the legitimate children of Abraham by their birth and their traditions—the "sons of the kingdom"—will be "thrown into the outer darkness."

This warning is addressed not only to Jews. It is addressed also to Christians. Does not the faith and love of people who have just discovered the gospel and scarcely yet dare to call themselves Christians often put to shame the inertia and the indifference of those who have nominally belonged to the Church from their infancy?

"He Took Our Infirmities" (8:14-17)

The third healing related in this chapter is that of the mother-in-law of Simon Peter. Jesus "touched her hand" and the fever left her (see Mark 1:29-31).

In verse 16, on the other hand, with regard to the demon-possessed, it is expressly said that Jesus cast them out "with a word." Of the numerous cases of possession cited in the Gospels, some suggest the psychic malady which today we call "split personality." The sick one identified himself with the evil spirit with which he felt possessed. There is no question that for Jesus and his contemporaries these were genuine cases of evil spirits who had seized men. It was the power of God which cast them out; hence the fright of the demoniacs at the approach of Jesus, for they immediately recognized who it was with whom they had to do (see Mark 1:23-24; 5:6-9; Matt. 8:29).

It is not necessary for us, in the name of science, to deny the reality of such powers at work in the world. We are still singularly ignorant of the relations between the spiritual world and the physical and psychological aspects of human nature. Jesus took very seriously the existence of hostile powers which were at work to destroy man. His ministry was a battle against these forces. In citing the word of Isaiah, "He took our infirmities and bore our diseases" (vs. 17; see Isa. 53:4), Matthew shows us not only the Messiah victorious over sin and death, but also the Suffering Servant who conquers only by taking on himself the weight of our misery as well as the burden of our faults. Each healing is a battle of the One whom Peter called "the Author of life" (Acts 3:15) against the forces of death.

Necessary Choices (8:18-22)

Jesus withdrew far from the crowd to the eastern shore of the lake, in the semi-Greek province of Decapolis. Several times we see him thus fleeing from superficial popularity. At this point the evangelist places two brief dialogues which Luke situates much later, at the time when Jesus was proceeding to Jerusalem (see Luke 9:51, 57-60). The words pronounced are practically the same in both stories, and at first glance they seem harsh. In the first instance, it seems that Jesus deliberately wanted to discourage the vocation of the one who offered himself to him. In the second, his demands superseded the most legitimate family obligations. Jesus desired that men engage in his service with full knowledge of what was involved, not with premature resolutions which lacked a realistic estimate of the cost involved (see also Luke 14:28-33). The Son of Man had chosen the way of poverty and insecurity. In this world, which belonged to him by right, he had nowhere to lay his head. The men who came to Jesus were faced with the question, Are you ready to follow on this way? Had he not, it may be replied, offered as an example to his disciples the lilies of the field and the birds of the air? (6:25-34). Had he not promised them that they would be protected? Yes, certainly, as he himself was protected, through all the shame and abandonment, even unto death. But this security does not spare one from struggle and suffering. It is given only to those who are ready to "leave all" for the love of God and his Kingdom. For

Jesus, all those who are not born into the life of the Kingdom, into the life of God, are "the dead" who bury their dead (vs. 22). To follow him is to *live*. The hour of decision, when it comes, demands obedience which is immediate and without conditions.

In this passage, we find on the lips of Jesus for the first time the expression "Son of man." This expression in Hebrew ordinarily designated *man* (Ezek. 2:3; 3:1, 4). Nevertheless, after Daniel (7:13-14), throughout the Jewish apocalypses the term had taken on a Messianic meaning. It designated the pre-existent, heavenly Judge, who would be revealed in the last days to inaugurate the new humanity.

In choosing this term to the exclusion of all others to designate himself, Jesus affirmed both the fullness of his humanity and the meaning of his coming. He is the Heavenly Man who will inaugurate the New Age. It is this sovereign authority which permits him to demand that men leave everything to follow him.

A Storm and a Healing
(8:23-34; see Mark 4:35-41; 5:1-20; Luke 8:22-39)

These two episodes, told in Mark with more detail, engraved themselves deeply on the minds of the disciples. The raging storm, with Jesus sleeping unconscious of the danger; their fear and his calm; the sea calmed by his voice as at that of God himself (see Ps. 107:23-30) gave rise to the question which came to their minds: Who is this man?

The next episode was at Gadara, where Jesus met two demoniacs (in Mark and Luke there is only one) whose raging madness terrified the country. In Jesus these recognize their enemy, the Son of God, whose coming is their condemnation and the precursor of the end of the age (the "time"). The rest of the story—the demons taking refuge in the swine which plunge into the sea—remains mysterious and we do not attempt to explain it. The people of the city begged Jesus to leave, doubtless because of the great loss which they had just experienced, the responsibility for which they attributed to him. Matthew does not reproduce the end of Mark's story, where Jesus made the healed demoniac his witness in the midst of the pagans (Mark 5:18-20). He tells only of the rejection of Jesus by the Gadarenes, their herds being more important to them than the salvation of a man. (On demon possession, see comment on 8:16.)

The Healing of the Paralytic
(9:1-8; see Mark 2:1-12; Luke 5:17-26)

This story contains, with respect to the preceding stories of healing, several characteristic traits. The first is the stress placed not so much on the faith of the sick man himself as on that of those who brought him to Jesus (see Mark 2:3-4). These men recognized the power of Jesus, expecting everything from him. In the second place, Jesus begins by proclaiming to the paralytic the forgiveness of his sins. In so doing, he goes directly to the heart of the predicament of this man; for his worst ill was not the wasting of his physical powers but the judgment of God which rested upon him. Whether the sickness was, in this particular case, a direct consequence of sin or not, for Jesus sickness and death are ultimately the fruits of sin, for God is the God of life. With sovereign authority, but also a great gentleness ("Take heart, my son"), Jesus lifted the interdict which rested on this man and declared to him that he had found pardon at the judgment seat of God. But who could say that, save God? The reaction of the scribes was immediate: "This man is blaspheming." The attitude of Jesus can be understood only if he is "the Son of man" in the Messianic sense—the heavenly Judge delegated by God to judge the actions and the thoughts of men at the last day.

Thus—and this is the third important trait of this story—the question already posed by all of Jesus' teaching and deeds is precisely put: Whence comes his authority? Who is this? (see 7:28; 8:27). At the same time the opposition looms which will one day condemn him as a blasphemer (vs. 3; see 26:65-66). The accusation is not yet formulated, but Jesus reads the thoughts of the scribes who surround him, and these thoughts are "evil." They spring up out of envy and not from a legitimate concern for the honor of God. Jesus responds by an act. The miracle of physical healing here is like the seal of God placed on the inner change wrought in the life of this man—the concrete manifestation of his pardon. The man obeyed, arose, and went home. The crowds were seized with fear and glorified God who had given such authority "to men." They did not yet know the importance of the term "Son of man" which Jesus had just used, or the unique character of his authority. But they recognized that God was at work in this man, and in that they rejoiced.

Two New Causes of Conflict
(9:9-17; see Mark 2:13-22; Luke 5:27-39)

The call of Matthew is told in few words. At the summons of
Jesus, he immediately left his profession, which was a very re-
munerative one (see Luke 19:2,8). He was a publican or tax officer, a collector of duty. One bought this position, a practice which
gave opportunity for much abuse. Furthermore, the tax collector
was in the employ of the detested Roman authority. His profession defiled him. For these reasons, publicans were regarded as a
species of outcast by strict Jews, who avoided all contact with
them. Jesus not only invited a publican to follow him, he also
made him one of the twelve Apostles (Matt. 10:3).

Further still, Jesus welcomed tax collectors and "sinners" (people of obviously bad life) to his table. They came spontaneously,
it seems, and gathered around him and his disciples. The pious
Jew, afraid of defiling himself, shunned inviting anyone to his
table who did not practice the ritual laws. The Pharisees strove
to constitute a community of "pure ones." Jesus thus breached all
the religious and social prejudices of his time. He made friends
of all these doubtful people. He accomplished the miracle that
they felt themselves "at home" with him.

The Pharisees were astonished. They did not question Jesus
directly, but spoke to the disciples. We see them here, full of a
scandalized solicitude: "Why does your teacher. . .?" Jesus, hearing their remarks, replied: "Those who are well have no need of
a physician, but those who are sick." It is for "the lost sheep" of
Israel that he has come (see 10:6; Luke 15:4-7). It is toward them
that his tenderness and his love carry him. They feel this, and
they come to him. There was in this no condescension on Jesus'
part, none of the self-righteousness which crushes the person to
whom one speaks.

Who are the "well" in this matter? Jesus recognizes in the Pharisees men who know the Law of God. He is not necessarily speaking ironically. The citation from Hosea (vs. 13; see Hosea 6:6)
expresses his profound thought. He who does not show mercy to
his neighbor multiplies sacrifices and offerings in vain. Jesus had
nothing to say to those who believed themselves to be righteous,
but spoke rather to those who knew themselves to be poor and
guilty and who had need of pardon. We find again in this teaching
the dominant thought of the whole Sermon on the Mount.

In the following episode (vss. 14-17) it is no longer Jesus and the Pharisees who have words with each other, but Jesus and the disciples of John the Baptist, who speak both for themselves and for the Pharisees. The debated question is that of fasting. It is to be noted that Jesus does not deny the legitimacy of fasting but its present appropriateness. The passage is weighted with Messianic significance, for he compares his coming to a wedding. For his disciples, the dawn of the Kingdom has come. It is a day of joy! How could they fast? The day will indeed come "when the bridegroom is taken away from them." This is a veiled allusion to his approaching death. The image of the wedding may seem strange to us. It strikes its roots into the Old Testament where the love of God is compared to that of a fiancé (Jer. 2:2; Ezek. 16:8). The image of a wedding is found again in relation to the royal banquet (Matt. 22:2-3). For Jesus to say that the bridegroom was there was to declare the arrival of the Messianic Age, a time of consummation and joy. And this note of joy remains the dominant one of the Apostolic Church, which awaited her Lord as a bride awaits her bridegroom (see John 3:29; Matt. 25:1; Rev. 19:6-8; 22:17).

The double parable of the Garment and the Wineskins sets forth the revolutionary element in the attitude of Jesus: the new times demand a new deportment, another style of life. The Messianic Age signifies a renewal of all things. The two images are suggestive. One does not sew the new onto the old; the fabric would tear. One does not pour new wine into old wineskins; it would burst them! Such is the dynamic of the Kingdom.

Do we know this revolutionary power of the gospel, this fresh and free manner of approaching men and of judging traditions, which gives to all things their true meaning?

A Raising and Three Healings (9:18-35)

The story of the raising of the daughter of the ruler of the synagogue is told in the Gospel by Mark in a much more lively and moving fashion (Mark 5:21-24, 35-43). Matthew retains only the essential facts: the faith of the father; the word of Jesus, "the girl is not dead but sleeping"; and the deed itself. The saying of Jesus has sometimes been interpreted as though this were a case of catalepsy. This does not seem to be the thought of the evangelist. Jesus is the great conqueror of death; so in this sense death, in the absolute and terrible meaning of the term—a definitive end—

does not exist. The dead "sleep" while awaiting the final resurrection (Dan. 12:2; see John 5:26-29; I Thess. 4:13-14). The raising of the girl, as all the healings wrought by Jesus, is a sign of
the omnipotence of God in the work of Jesus, a prior sign of that
Kingdom where sickness and death will be no more.

The healing of the woman (vss. 20-22), in Matthew as in Mark,
is inserted into the story concerning the raising of the child (see
Mark 5:25-34). Once again we have in Matthew only a very ab-
breviated echo of Mark. The story here lacks the deeply human
note—the agony of the woman that her illness rendered her "unclean," her daring to touch Jesus, the reaction of Jesus to her
touch. But in both stories, Jesus sees in the woman's faith the
cause of her healing. She had believed on him, and she had been
heard.

The story of the healing of the blind men (vss. 27-31) is found
in almost identical form in 20:29-34, which may be a second telling of the same event. The writer likely places it here because the
cure was a characteristic sign of the Messianic Age: "the eyes of
the blind shall see" (Isa. 29:18; see also 35:5; 42:7). Physical
blindness is often regarded as a symbol of spiritual blindness (see
John 9). Up until now the total behavior of Jesus, including his
words and his acts, manifests an authority which could only be
that of the One sent by God; but his Messiahship has not been
recognized as such by those whom he has healed. The blind men,
by calling him "Son of David," proclaim his royalty. They thus
unveil the hidden meaning of everything which has already been
related. Jesus bids them to be silent. The Messianic secret must
be kept until the ministry of Jesus is completed (see 16:20). Jesus
himself will disclose it at the final trial (26:63-64).

Once more the evangelist underlines the *faith* of those who
are healed. This faith consists in recognizing in Jesus the One sent
from God, the almighty Master of life and death. The question
posed for the two blind men is likewise posed for us: "Do you believe" in his power?

Verses 32-34 tell of a "dumb demoniac." To be dumb is to be
tragically cut off from one's fellow men; and this illness was
viewed as the work of a demon. The crowds marveled at this cure.
But the opposition was there, sullenly saying, "He casts out demons by the prince of demons." This theme will be developed
later (12:22-30). It is here as an announcement of a deep hostility which will eventually stand out more and more vigorously.

Verse 35 sums up the activity of Jesus in practically the same words as those by which the writer had introduced the first stage in his public ministry (4:23).

CONTINUATION OF THE GALILEAN MINISTRY: FOUR DISCOURSES
Matthew 9:36—16:12

The plan of these chapters is less clear than that of the preceding ones. The narrative opens with the call and sending out of the twelve Apostles and leads up to the confession of Peter (16: 13-20). The evangelist groups the teaching of Jesus in four "discourses": (1) instructions addressed to the disciples (10:5—11:1); (2) a discourse concerning John the Baptist and the unbelief of "this generation" (ch. 11); (3) controversies with the Pharisees (ch. 12); and (4) a series of parables (ch. 13). From 13:53 to 16:12 the order of the narrative follows that of Mark (see Mark 6:1—8:21). It is a series of episodes—miracles, and new discussions with the Pharisees—which reveal anew, on the one hand, the power of Jesus and his success with the crowds, and on the other hand, the hostility to which he is exposed.

The Mission of the Twelve (9:36—11:1)

The evangelist has grouped in chapter 10 some teachings relating to the disciples, of which some are peculiar to him (10:5-8, 23) while others are found also in Mark or Luke in different contexts. All three Gospels mention the call of the Twelve and their being sent on mission, but the instructions mentioned in Mark 6:7-11 and Luke 9:1-5 are much briefer. On the other hand, there is a marked parallelism between Matthew 10:1-15 and the mission of the Seventy which is related by Luke alone (Luke 10:1-12). In Matthew, however, the mission is centered on Israel, while in Luke it is situated at the entering into Samaria and seems directed toward the evangelization of the Gentiles (70 is the symbolic number of the nations). This difference corresponds to the precise aim of each of these Gospels.

The Time of Harvest (9:36-38)

Crowds thronged Jesus in such numbers that he was obliged from time to time to cross to the other side of the lake (8:18; 14:

13). The Gospel pictures him as moved with "compassion" before
this intense yearning of people who were distressed, thirsting for
deliverance, languishing and dejected, "like sheep without a shepherd." God's people no longer had sure guides, but were at the
mercy of exploiters or of blind leaders. The image of the flock
is taken from the Old Testament: God is called the "Shepherd of
Israel" (Ps. 80:1); this title was also given to the leaders to whom
God entrusted the care of his flock (Num. 27:15-17); the wicked
shepherds who allowed Israel to be "scattered upon the mountains" are severely judged (I Kings 22:17; Ezek. 34; Jer. 23:1-4).
The coming Messiah, the New David, had as his mission precisely
to gather and to heal the scattered flock (Ezek. 34:10, 23-24; Jer.
23:5). It is with a view to this "gathering" that Jesus has come;
and that is the mission which he is going to entrust to his disciples (see Matt. 10:6; 15:24; 18:12-14; John 10).

"The harvest is plentiful, but the laborers are few" (vs. 37; Luke
10:2). The image of the "harvest" calls to mind the decisive moment when the grain is cut, gathered, sorted—that is to say, the
end of the world, the Judgment (see 3:12; 13:30, 39-40). In Jesus,
God calls; the gathering and the sorting of the end-time has begun. But there is an overwhelming disproportion between the im-
mensity of the field and the small number of the harvesters. Jesus
did not say, as he might have been expected to, "Recruit harvesters," but "Pray . . . the Lord of the harvest . . ." His first watch-
word in the face of the needs of the hour was an invitation to
prayer. To be sure, this was a call to active prayer, which implies
a total expendability. But the harvest is the work of God.

The forlornness of the crowds—without a shepherd or actually
delivered over to false shepherds—is perhaps greater today than
ever. Do we sense the immeasurable yearning of a world that knows
not where it is going? Are we moved by its distress as Jesus was?

The Call and Sending of the Twelve (10:1-16)

The choice of the twelve Apostles is described with more precision in Mark 3:13-19. The choice rests entirely on the decision
of Jesus himself (see Mark 3:13; John 15:16). The number
"twelve" is certainly a symbol which brings to mind the twelve
tribes of Israel. Here is the New Israel, the Israel of the end-time,
which, according to the Messianic hope, would serve as a rallying
center for all the nations. Hence, it is on Israel that Jesus is going
to concentrate at first (see Isa. 2:2-3; 60; Jer. 3:17).

The term "apostle" means "one sent," but one sent with a mandate to speak and act in the name of the one who sent him. Jesus gave *power* to his disciples to preach (vs. 7) and to heal (vss. 1 and 8) in his name. They could do nothing by themselves, they could only give what they had received. But the transfer of power is so real that to reject them would be to reject Jesus himself.

The names of the Apostles are given. The vocation of five of them is mentioned (4:18-22; 9:9); that of the others remains unknown. Among them was a zealot, Simon the Cananaean (the term "zealot" signifies "zeal"; see Luke 6:15), an adherent of the nationalistic sect; perhaps Judas Iscariot belonged to it also. The choice of these men by Jesus remains heavy with mystery, for even at this early moment we are informed that one of the twelve intimate ones later betrayed him.

The instruction to "go nowhere among the Gentiles, and enter no town of the Samaritans" astonishes us in the light of such words as those cited in Matthew 8:11-13. But it is understood quite clearly by those who take seriously the vocation of Israel in the plan of God. There is no exclusivism involved; it is rather a matter of priority in time. It is toward the people who have received the promises, who have been charged with being God's witnesses among the nations, that Jesus turns first. This is why his appeals to the leaders of this people will have particular urgency and severity. This is also why he addresses himself with such marked solicitude to the "lost sheep" of the flock which God had declared his own. The hour of final decision has sounded, and all the children of Israel must be warned of it, for nothing less is involved than the coming of the Kingdom, that coming which the most faithful among them have believed in and waited for from century to century (10:7; compare Luke 10:8-11). Here again this coming must be proclaimed both in *words* (vs. 7) and in *acts* (vs. 8). The Kingdom of God comes with *power*.

The grace of God is a free gift and ought to be proclaimed "without pay." On the other hand, the worker for God is to count on the necessities of life being given him; he is to have food and lodging.

Why did Jesus demand of his first missionaries such radical privation? How could they travel about this rugged country without sandals and staff? It is important to note that the text of Matthew here goes beyond the thought of Mark precisely at these

two points (see Mark 6:8-9). Is it possible that this is a reflec-
tion of a Jewish ritual prescription which demanded that one not
present himself on the mountain of God (the Temple) "with staff,
shoes, purse, or dusty feet"? The meaning would then be: "Behave yourself in all things as it becomes one to behave himself
in the presence of God, in a prayerful attitude, humble and exposed; for the whole earth is his Temple." At any rate, it is still
true that the disciple of the Son of Man should present himself
to those whom he evangelizes as a "pauper," clothed only with
the power of God.

This passage poses a difficult question to missionaries in every
age. Should they appeal to oriental hospitality, which finds it
completely natural to welcome and to lodge a man of God? This
can never be a question of external rules, of a forced asceticism.
The attitude of Paul shows clearly that this is not a matter of an
absolute rule. He did not hesitate, in certain circumstances, voluntarily to deprive himself of this gratuitous hospitality which
he considered at other times as a right (see I Cor. 9:3-18). He
earned his bread by the sweat of his brow in order to safeguard
the freedom of the gospel. With regard to material goods he
gave evidence of a magnificent liberty (see Phil. 4:10-13). What
must be retained of Jesus' instructions is, first, the complete casting of every need on the Father, which permits us to face the
privations inherent in every authentic ministry without being
"anxious" (see 6:25-34). Then, too, there must be retained the
simplicity of life which makes the one sent a "neighbor" to those
to whom God sends him, integrates him into their manner of
life, and disposes him to receive as well as to give.

It is this expendability, this subjection to others, which stands
out again in Jesus' command that they stay in the same house
once they have entered it (vs. 11). What is meant by a man
"worthy" to receive the disciples? A Jew faithful in the practice
of his faith? The expression is a little surprising. Did not Jesus
enter into the homes of publicans as well as those of Pharisees?
Should we see in this reference a tradition of the Church
rather than a word of the Lord? (This note is absent from Luke
10:5.) Nevertheless, Jesus may have enjoined a certain discernment.

The familiar Hebrew salutation was, "Peace be with you." That
which was too often only a form becomes here a word clothed
with power. It effects that which it says. It saves, it heals. Yet

it is necessary that it be "received"; if not, it "returns" to the one who has pronounced it. But it is not without effect, for it judges the one who has rejected it (see Isa. 55:10-11).

The coming of the Kingdom of God is presented once more as a decisive moment which demands an immediate decision. The expression "shake off the dust from your feet" signifies that the responsibility of refusal rests entirely on those who have thus been called and have not responded. The hour of judgment sounds for them as it had sounded of old for Sodom and Gomorrah, consumed by the fire of God (see Gen. 18:20-21; 19:22-28). Corrupt though they were, Sodom and Gomorrah were less guilty than the towns of Palestine, for their time had been a time of ignorance, while today the Kingdom of God is revealed with power and those who reject it choose deliberately to remain in death (vs. 15; see 11:23-24; Luke 10:12; 19:41-44).

Jesus compares his disciples to sheep sent into the midst of wolves (10:16; Luke 10:3). He has no illusions about the jungle which is the world; he knows that this world is cruel and violent. He delivers his own disarmed to the blows of the enemy, for their arms are of another order. He anticipates that they will be bitten and torn to pieces. Was he not himself constantly in battle with slander, intrigue, and hate?

To this saying Matthew adds another which he alone records: "be wise as serpents and innocent as doves." The dove is a symbol of purity and innocence; the serpent of cleverness and craftiness. The paradox which unites these opposites shows that the simplicity of the heart ought not to exclude shrewdness and prudence. One must not seek martyrdom; there will be times when it is necessary to flee danger (see Matt. 10:23; 24:16), and other times when it is necessary to defend one's self with the weapons of the wisdom of God (Matt. 10:20; see Luke 21:14-15), and still other times when it is necessary to consent to the last sacrifice, to be a "sheep that before its shearers is dumb" (Isa. 53:7; Acts 8:32-35).

The Sufferings Which Await the Disciples (10:17-23)

The sayings which Matthew inserts here (vss. 17-22) reproduce exactly those which are found in the last discourse of Jesus on the persecutions to come and the end of the age, where they seem to be more in place (see Mark 13:9-13; Luke 21:12-19). In fact, the disciples encountered no persecution in the course of this

first mission (compare the testimony of Luke on the mission of
the seventy; Luke 10:17-18).

It must be remembered that the Gospels have no rigorous
chronological concern; they are not lives of Jesus but rather are
digests of the essential themes of his teaching. In particular instances they are designed to prepare Jesus' followers for the
struggles to which they will be exposed. Verses 17-18 describe
exactly the double persecution which the Church of the first days
knew: persecution by the Jews and persecution by the Roman
authorities. Those who are thus exposed in persecution for the
love of Christ do not need to be in distress over the testimony
they will have to render. God himself, when the hour comes,
will speak by their mouth. This is a magnificent assurance given
to the persecuted in every age. At the hour when the adversary
attacks the believers with all his force, the Holy Spirit is present
and speaks with power. This is the promise of the Lord; the
entire history of the Church confirms it. But attacks will come not
from the outside only. The times of struggle will set members of
the same family against one another; they will go so far as to
inform against one another. The ideological struggles of our own
epoch confirm this terrible verdict.

Just as Jesus Christ was hated because of the divine truth of
which he was the bearer and the witness, so his disciples will be
exposed to hatred because of him (vs. 22; see John 15:18-20).
For "men"—the natural men of hardened heart—do not want
God. His word illuminates with too penetrating a light the deepest
secrets of their hearts. The more it resounds with power, the more
they wish to silence it. Jesus has prepared his disciples for this
conflict from the beginning of his ministry; persecution is the
lot of the "prophets" of God (5:11-12), that is to say, the authentic witnesses through whom the voice of God makes itself
heard. Blessed are those who hold firm to the end! Jesus' warning concludes with an appeal for perseverance; for in the furnace
of persecution, he says later (24:12-13), the love of many will
"grow cold."

Verse 23 is a practical counsel on flight. In a period of persecution it is vain to expose oneself uselessly; the duty of remaining
or leaving becomes a matter of discernment. Thus we see the
Christians at a given moment—with the exception of the Apostles
—fleeing Jerusalem (Acts 8:1-4) and spreading the gospel far
and wide. We see Paul fleeing several times in order to pursue

his ministry elsewhere. Jesus himself stole away from his adversaries until "his hour" was come; then he went deliberately to death.

The end of verse 23 poses a difficult question. Did Jesus mean to say that the coming of the Son of Man—the end of the age—was so near that his disciples would not have completed the evangelization of Palestine before the last hour would have sounded? Numerous texts show that he believed the end of the age to be near (compare Mark 9:1; Matt. 24:32-34), while affirming that no one knew the hour of it (Mark 13:32; Matt. 24:36). At the time when the evangelist cited this word the first generation had passed, Jerusalem had in all probability been destroyed, and the gospel had been announced to the nations "throughout the whole world" (compare Matt. 24:14). But Palestine in its entirety had not been converted to the new faith, and it was to its inhabitants, it would seem, that this Gospel was addressed. Is it possible that Matthew gives to the saying of Jesus another meaning than its original meaning, and recognized with Paul that the final conversion of the Jewish people would happen only at the end of the age? (Rom. 11:25-32). Or did Matthew faithfully reproduce this word of his Master just as he received it, without seeking to pierce the mystery of it? Let us have no more presumption than he!

Master and Disciples (10:24-33; see Luke 12:2-9)

The meaning of verses 24-25 is clear; the disciple cannot expect to be treated better than his master (see 10:22 and John 15:18-21). If men have not hesitated to slander the Master, so much the more will they slander the disciples. Jesus plays here on the word "Be-elzebul," which in Aramaic means "the Lord of the house." The disciples belong to the family, to the house of Jesus. If they have given him the name of Devil, how could this title not be extended to them? Let us note in passing this subtle irony.

The saying on the hidden things which will be revealed is found in Mark 4:22 in connection with the lamp put under a bushel and in Luke 12:2-3 in connection with the hypocrisy of the Pharisees. Here it is a sequel to what is said of slander. The disciples ought not to fear the judgments expressed about them, or the truth concerning them and concerning their accusers will one day be revealed. Everything which today remains secret will

be unveiled. What Jesus is has not yet been revealed, and only
the disciples know the mystery hidden in his coming (compare
13:11). But that which he confides to them in private, in a
veiled manner ("in the dark"), must be proclaimed openly when
the day has come (that is to say, after his death and resurrection).
That will be the hour of the public confession of faith, this confession which is to lead to martyrdom. For men can kill only the
body, they cannot kill the soul; that is to say, they cannot kill
the true life, that life which God alone gives and he alone can
take away. It is solely his judgment that one must fear. If the life
of a sparrow is in the hand of God, how much more ours! This
concern of God for the least living being—how much greater is
it for his children! If it is proper to tremble over offending him,
it is because he is "our Father" by whom each hair of our heads
is numbered. To fear, to doubt, even to betray the love which he
has manifested to us, to deny him—veritable death consists in
such things as these, and it is before this death that it is necessary
to tremble.

This saying leads quite naturally to the following, on the confession of faith (vss. 32-33; compare Mark 8:38). Jesus declares
that it is not enough to believe on him in some secret way; it is
necessary to confess him *openly* before men.

What is it to confess Jesus Christ? It is to proclaim by our
words and our acts that he is truly our Lord, the One to whom
we belong, the sovereign Master of our lives. It is to announce
his salvation to men, for such a pardon is only truly received if
we are eager to pass it on to others (compare I Peter 2:9-10;
Rom. 10:14-15; II Cor. 4:5-6; 5:14-15). We are called to "confess" his name (Phil. 2:11; I Tim. 6:12-13; compare Acts 4:9-
20). It was the courageous confession of the faith which permitted the expansion of Christianity in the first century; it is this
same courageous confession which has drawn persecution upon
Christians. Jesus "will acknowledge" before his Father—that is
to say, will recognize—his own who have confessed him by word
and in heart before men. But he will not acknowledge those who
have denied him, whether the denial be by their acts, their words,
or their silences.

Not Peace But a Sword (10:34—11:1)

Verses 34-39 resume the theme begun earlier (vss. 21-22) of
the struggles which the disciples will have to endure, even in their

own families (see Luke 12:51-53). Verse 34 shocks us by the violence of its paradox: "I have not come to bring peace, but a sword." Can it be the Christ of the Beatitudes, the proclaimer of peace, who speaks thus? Yes, it is; for to announce the peace of God is to denounce all false ideas of peace, which are only frightful caricatures of it, as when the false prophets say, "Peace, peace," when there is no peace (Jer. 6:14). What passes under the name of "peace" is often only a mask which covers indiscriminately truth and error, justice and injustice. Such peace God loathes (Rev. 3:15-16). Jesus has come to disturb our false quietude, to tear to pieces with the sword of his word all the masks by which we cover ourselves (see Heb. 4:12-13). And some cruel rendings may be the result. The hour may come when the demand to "leave all" may take a concrete meaning which our near relatives cannot accept. Jesus himself knew such a painful rupture of family ties (see Mark 3:21; John 7:5). He knew that the disciples would also experience it. Jesus demands that he be first in the affection of those who belong to him; their love for him must take primacy over the most legitimate of affections —the love of children for their parents and of parents for their children. This demand can be understood only if love for Jesus and love for God are one and the same thing. In this passage it is the Lord who speaks, clothed with the sovereign authority of God himself. Every Jew knows that to love God is the first commandment. God alone can demand unconditional obedience. Jesus gives his life for his own. To be "worthy" of him is to be ready to follow him, even though it should be to the ignominious death of the cross.

Verse 38 is found also in Matthew 16:24 (compare Mark 8:34; Luke 9:23; 14:27). The cross is not only a symbol of death, it represents the humiliated condition of a slave. This condition Jesus had made his own. And here again, the disciple is not above his Master. To follow him is to be exposed to humiliation and outrage. This saying is bound to the following, which is also a key saying cited in all the Gospels and repeated twice in some of them (Matt. 10:39; 16:25; Mark 8:35; Luke 9:24-25; 17:33; John 12:25). To "find" one's life may be to draw back from the final sacrifice of physical life and for that reason to deny one's faith. But the term has a larger meaning than that. It may mean allowing some dear affections or some human considerations, of whatever sort, to close for us the way of obedience. To do this is

to believe one's self to be living but in reality to be separated
from God and thus given over to death. This is to live in illusion.
It is to prefer the immediate and transient goods of the present
life to the call of Christ who alone can make us "alive" in the
biblical sense of the word, as children of the Kingdom.

To the radical demand corresponds the promise, equally radical. Jesus will consider what is done to one of those whom he has
sent as done to himself. To receive them is to receive him, and to
receive him is to receive the Father who sent him. This leads us
back to the initial declaration of the whole chapter: there is a
transmission of power and authority from the one who sends to
those who are sent (compare 10:1). They do not act in their
own name. They give nothing which they have not first received.
Those who receive them as "prophets" thereby acknowledge the
words which they speak as words of God—for the prophet is "the
mouth of God" (see Jer. 1:9; 15:19)—and consequently they are
blessed. Those who receive them as "righteous"—that is, as faithful believers—will receive the recompense which accrues to them.
And those even who give them a cup of cold water for the love
of Jesus will be blessed by God for this act of love. Note the
term "little ones" applied to the disciples. The missionaries of
the Early Church were often from among the humble, the arti-
sans, the tradesmen, the slaves, who announced the good news
around them. The entire Gospel by Matthew (see the Beatitudes;
compare also 11:25) shows that it is the humble of heart to
whom Jesus confides the proclamation of his Kingdom. A benediction rests on these ministries, often obscure, as well as on
those who, in receiving them, reap the fruits thereof.

Discourse Concerning John the Baptist (11:2-30)

This narrative has as its point of departure an inquiry of John
the Baptist sent to Jesus (11:2-6), an inquiry which is the occasion of a declaration of Jesus about the person and work of
the Baptist (vss. 7-15) and a judgment on the unbelieving crowds
who received neither John's message nor his own (vss. 16-24).
But some have believed; hence the discourse concludes with a
giving of thanks by Jesus and a clear affirmation of his divine
Sonship and of the salvation which he brings (vss. 25-30).

John's Question and Jesus' Reply (11:2-6; see Luke 7:18-23)

"He who is to come" is a classic expression, somewhat veiled, to designate the Messiah. People are often astonished that the Baptist had such a doubt, in view of what has been said about him previously (3:11-15). It must be remembered, however, that in the thought of the Baptist the coming of the Messiah coincided with the Last Judgment, when the just would be delivered and the wicked destroyed (3:12). Then, too, John is in prison for having had the courage of the prophets (see 14:3-12). And "the Messiah" remains silent. He seems impotent. Evil continues to triumph. What John's disciples have reported to him is not completely reassuring. Could it be that Jesus is only a prophet like himself, a forerunner and not the Messiah-Judge of the end-time? John honestly posed this question to Jesus.

Jesus replies with deeds. John would immediately grasp their significance; for they are the "signs" announced by the prophets (Isa. 35:5-6), signs which even go beyond what had been prophesied, for Jesus mentions the healing of lepers and the raising of the dead. But more important than all the healings is the fact that "the poor have good news preached to them" (see Isa. 61:1). The signs of the Kingdom are there. But it comes otherwise than John had foreseen; no fire from heaven falls on the wicked. This mystery of the Kingdom which comes in a manner both real and hidden, Jesus does not explain.

His works testify to Jesus for those who "understand." "Blessed is he who takes no offense at me." This "offense" is the mystery of the Son's coming under the form of the Servant. This is the scandal of the Cross (see Matt. 16:21-23; I Cor. 1:22-25).

Jesus' Declaration Concerning John the Baptist (11:7-19; see Luke 7:24-28; 16:16; 7:31-35)

The crowds had to face the questions of the origin and the relation between these two "prophets," at the same time so alike and so different. This had already produced some discussions between their respective disciples (see Matt. 9:14). Paul later found some men who knew only the baptism of John (Acts 18:25; 19:1-5). This indicates that the problem remained real in the Early Church, and it is not by accident that all the evangelists underline the role of the Baptist as *forerunner* (Matt. 3; Mark 1:3-8; Luke 3:15-17; John 1:6-8, 19-40; 3:22-30).

The words spoken by Jesus, as they are reported to us in Matthew 11, are designed to throw light on a latent question: What did Jesus himself say about the person and work of John the Baptist? The testimony which Jesus rendered to the Baptist is as explicit as it could be. John was no changeable man, a reed swinging in the wind, a courtier looking for an easy life. (Was this perhaps an ironic remark directed toward the detractors of John?) Those who had gone to find him in the desert knew him: it was to an authentic prophet they had gone. But his greatness surpassed that of the prophets, for he had been the announcer of the coming Kingdom, the herald who opened the way for the King (Mal. 3:1; Isa. 40:3). Among all those born of women, there was none greater than he!

Here follows immediately a word which baffles us: "yet he who is least in the kingdom of heaven is greater than he" (vs. 11). This text sets over against the natural birth another—the birth from above (compare John 3:3-5). John stands on the threshold of the New Age, he announces it; in Jesus it has come. John is the last great figure of the Old Covenant and in a fashion he wins the Kingdom by main force, by asceticism and heroic obedience (vs. 12). But the New Covenant of which Jesus is the incarnation is a Covenant of grace, and marks a new beginning. This saying is not a judgment on the person of John, and certainly does not prejudge his eternal destiny; but it traces a clear line of demarcation between the former time and the New Age which Jesus inaugurates. John is the "Elijah who is to come" (vs. 14; see Mal. 4:5-6). To say this, for those who were able to understand, was to say that now, in the Person of Jesus, the Kingdom of God had come. And this coming, as has been seen earlier, is good and joyous news; it is the announcement of salvation.

The following sayings (vss. 16-19) are a melancholy declaration. The crowds are like changeable children who always demand a kind of music other than that which is offered them. They will neither dance with those who dance nor sing lamentations with those who play a funeral dirge. John practiced austere abstinence and they accused him of being demon-possessed. Jesus came "eating and drinking" and they charged him with being fond of wild living, with having evil companions (compare Matt. 9:10-15). They objected to John because of his asceticism and to Jesus because of the freedom with which he used the good things of this world and because he fraternized with sinners. Jesus did not appear to his contemporaries as a man austere and detached from the world, but as a man open to joy, free of prejudice, truly a man among men.

Verse 19b indicates that, however different John and Jesus were, the wisdom of God spoke through them both. It was necessary to understand their twofold message—a message of repentance and a message of joy; for only he who has first understood and accepted condemnation can grasp the joy of salvation. "Wisdom is justified by her deeds" (Luke says, "by . . . her children," 7:35). The wisdom of God does not work among men in vain. Over against the ingratitude of the many is set the faith of those who have understood and believed. By them God is "justified"—that is, recognized for what he is.

The Guilt of the Galilean Cities (11:20-24)

The guilt of the cities of Galilee, of which only three are mentioned, lies in the fact that they have been witnesses of the miracles and the message of Jesus. The hour of decision has sounded for them, and in refusing to repent they bring on themselves the judgment of God. For those who do not welcome it, the good news becomes condemnation (compare John 3:17-21). Had such a message of salvation been proclaimed within the walls of even pagan cities such as Tyre and Sidon, they would have put on "sackcloth and ashes." The most severe word is addressed to Capernaum, for Jesus had lived and had done many of his miracles there (8:5-13, 14-17; 9:1-8; compare Luke 4:23). Will Capernaum be able to boast at the last day of having sheltered the Son of Man? On the contrary, it will be "brought down to Hades." It will be judged in proportion to that which it has received—judged more severely than Sodom, which was regarded by the Jews as accursed (see 10:15).

This warning must be taken seriously. Those who have never heard the name of Jesus Christ will be more readily pardoned than those who honor him with their lips but have never taken seriously either the judgment or the salvation of God.

Of the Mystery of Revelation (11:25-30)

Matthew concludes the whole discourse here by three very important sayings in which Jesus reveals explicitly that of which he heretofore has spoken only in veiled terms—the unique character of his Person and mission.

The first two sayings are placed in Luke's Gospel immediately after the return of the disciples, who were full of joy because of the answers to prayer they had experienced on their mission. Jesus, we are told, "rejoiced in the Holy Spirit" and rendered thanks (Luke 10:17-24).

The context of Matthew is very different. Jesus has just spoken of a defeat. From this fact his praise takes on a more general and more profound meaning. God is "Lord of heaven and earth," who can be known only by those to whom he pleases to reveal himself. And the mystery of his revelation consists in this—that "these things" (meaning the things of his Kingdom) remain hidden to "the wise and understanding" and revealed "to babes." Who are these wise and understanding? Without doubt Jesus is thinking of the scribes, the doctors of the Law, whose suspicion pursues him from place to place; of all those who are shut up to their own wisdom and because of this are incapable of recognizing God when he comes to them. The Old Testament had previously denounced the false wisdom of the "wise" (Jer. 8:8-9; 9:23-24; Isa. 29:14). And Paul, for whom the Cross had shattered all human wisdom, later took up the saying of Isaiah and set over against all human wisdom the holy folly of God, "a secret and hidden wisdom" (I Cor. 1:18-31; 2:6-8).

Who are the "babes"? They are those humble, unimportant people, very ignorant in the eyes of the scholars and the "wise," who have believed in Jesus and have left all to follow him; those simple folk to whom God, in his broad benevolence, has been gracious in revealing his Kingdom and declaring himself their Father. Such is the purpose of God. It is manifested in the rejection of some as well as in the election of others. And this purpose fills Jesus with adoration: "Yea, Father, for such was thy gracious will."

The following saying (vs. 27) reveals the mystery of the Person of Jesus himself. To be sure, we have seen him throughout the Gospel speaking and acting with a sovereign authority; he has several times intimated the unique character of his mission. But here, for the first time, it is disclosed that we are standing before the unique Son of the Father, the One to whom all things have been delivered, the One whom the Father alone knows and who alone knows the Father.

Reflect a moment on this word "know." In the Bible it never means merely intellectual knowledge, but rather a living rela-

tionship which engages the entire person. For the believer of
the Old Testament to be known by God was both a mercy and a
terror (Ps. 139); to know him was the supreme good (Exod. 33:
12-13; Hosea 2:19-20; 6:6; Isa. 11:9; Jer. 31:33-34). The knowledge of God is central in the Messianic hope, the great characteristic of the New Age.

In proclaiming that the Father had delivered all things to him
Jesus was confiding the secret of his authority. In his Person it is
the Father who speaks and acts (compare John 5:19-27). No one
save the Father knows the Son. Not only is he misunderstood by
his enemies, but his disciples themselves do not know who he is.
Only the Father knows him, and only the Father can reveal him
(see 16:17). Nor does anyone know the Father save the Son "and
any one to whom the Son chooses to reveal him" (compare John
1:18; 14:6-10). The mystery of the divine Sonship announced
here will be manifested in all its power and fullness only after
the Resurrection (see 28:18-19).

The saying recorded in verses 28-30 belongs to the peculiar
treasure of the Gospel by Matthew. It is a word of consolation
to all the weary and burdened of the world. Jesus offers them
rest. Men spoke readily of "the yoke of the law" and that yoke
was heavy (see 23:4; Acts 15:10). Jesus declares that his yoke is
"easy."

Why? Because Jesus inflicts no yoke on his own which he has
not carried himself, before them, with them, for them. He is the
Suffering Servant who does not break the "bruised reed" (see Isa.
42:2-4), and who has taken on himself all the burdens of men
(see Isa. 53:2-5; Matt. 8:17).

His teachings are inseparable from his Person; he is "gentle and
lowly in heart" (vs. 29; see 5:3-5); he made himself poor with the
poor. And what he enjoins, he gives. He has come to give to his
own "a new heart"; and the law written in the heart becomes a
yoke both easy and light (Jer. 31:33; Ezek. 36:26; I John 5:3-4).
This illuminates all his teaching, which if separated from his Person would seem heavy with impossible demands (Matt. chs. 5-7).

Discussions with the Pharisees (12:1-50)

The evangelist has grouped here a series of events in the course
of which the conflict between Jesus and the Pharisees is shown
to be more and more insoluble, to the point where the Pharisees

plot to kill him (vs. 14). They accuse Jesus of violating the Sabbath (12:1-15), and of being an instrument of the Devil (12:22-
37); they demand from him a convincing miracle (12:38-45).
They clearly are calling in question his Messianic claims. Matthew introduces into these stories a quotation from Isaiah which
throws light on their meaning.

The Son of Man, Lord of the Sabbath
(12:1-21; see Mark 2:23—3:6)

The first cause of conflict seems to us to be very innocent.
The disciples of Jesus, being hungry, pluck some grains of wheat.
That for which they are reproached is not the plucking of the
grains of wheat (for which they would probably be reproached
today!) but the doing of it on the Sabbath. For such an act was
considered "work." It must be remembered with what strictness
the Sabbath was observed in Judaism. The Sabbath law was
sacred among all. During the Maccabean period there were
Jews who permitted themselves to be massacred without defense
rather than violate the Sabbath (I Macc. 2:31-38). Hunger, therefore, could not justify such a violation—such was the argument
of the Pharisees. Jesus replied with two scriptural arguments,
the one taken from the life of David (see I Sam. 21:1-6), the
other from the law concerning the sacrifices offered in the Temple
on the Sabbath (see Num. 28:9-10). His reply had meaning only
if in his Person there was one present who was greater than David
and greater than the Temple (vs. 6). The term "Son of man" must
be understood in its Messianic sense: Jesus is the Son of David,
the sovereign Judge who inaugurates the end-time. He is, therefore, Lord of the Sabbath.

But in acting as he did, he is faithful to the spirit of the Old
Covenant. He fulfilled the word which God had spoken by the
mouth of Hosea: "I desire steadfast love and not sacrifice"
(Hosea 6:6). What is piety without love?

The episode that follows turns on a healing done by Jesus on
the Sabbath. This theme is frequently taken up in the Gospels
(see Mark 3:1-6; Luke 6:6-11; 14:1-6; John 5:1-16; 9:1-14). For
Jesus each healing is a victory of God over Satan, a sign announcing the coming Kingdom, the great final rest—that rest of
God which it was the precise mission of the Sabbath to recall
and to announce (Gen. 2:1-3; compare Heb. 4:3-10). Is it not the
day par excellence on which it is legitimate "to do good"? (vs.

12). To these Pharisees who were so anxious to keep the letter of
the Law Jesus replies, perhaps not without a barb of irony, that
when one of their sheep falls into a pit on the Sabbath they do
not hesitate to pull it out. Is not a man of much more worth?
(see Luke 14:1-6). Jesus is scandalized and grieved by the hardness of their hearts (see Mark 3:5).

We could be astonished that a simple healing could provoke
the anger of the Pharisees to the point where they plot the death
of Jesus from that moment (12:14; see Mark 3:6; Luke 6:11;
John 5:16). But it must be understood that Jesus put their whole
theology—even more, their whole authority—in question. Given
the ascendancy of Jesus over the crowds and the sovereignty
which proceeds from his words and his acts, if he is not the
Messiah he is an impostor, a blasphemer. And it is indeed this
last question which the following stories raise.

Matthew prepares us, as he has done several times before, by
inserting into the text a sort of confession of faith (vss. 15-21).
Yes, Jesus is indeed the Anointed of God, the Messiah announced
by the prophets. But what he is must as yet remain secret (vs.
16). He comes, according to the ancient prophecy (see Isa. 42:
1-4), under the form of a Servant. The Spirit of God rests on
him. He will not fail until he has made justice triumph on the
earth. He is the hope of the nations. But he comes without pomp.
He flees noisy manifestations. He is merciful. He does not break
the bruised reed. He does not extinguish the wick which still
smokes. It is to the "little people," those defeated by life, that his
solicitude is directed.

Thus little by little there emerges before us the figure of the
King who comes under the form of the suffering and unrecognized
Servant. He gives life to others only by offering up his own (see
Isa. 52:13—53:12).

The Blind and Dumb Demoniac (12:22-37; see Mark 3:20-30)

This passage poses the decisive question: Who is Jesus? The
crowds ask: Can this man who is so powerful over demons be
the Son of David—that is, the Messiah? Who else could do such
miracles? That which is not within the power of man is within the
power of God—or of demons. For the characteristic of demons
is to imitate the work of God. Thus the reply of the Pharisees
is to be expected: "It is only by Be-elzebul, the prince of demons,
that this man casts out demons."

Jesus combats them on their own ground by showing that their reasoning is fallacious and illogical. Would Satan destroy his own work? He is certainly too intelligent to do that! A kingdom divided against itself cannot stand. It is the logic of evil that its works carry the mark of their author. But whose imprint do the deliverances wrought by Jesus carry? If their origin is in Satan, from what source are the healings wrought by the disciples of the Pharisees? Does not their accusation turn on them? Hence, it is by their "sons" that the accusers will be judged.

But if, on the contrary, it is by the Spirit of God that Jesus has power to cast out demons, this signifies that the Kingdom of God has made an irruption into the world. It signifies, in other terms, that the hour of God has sounded, that the Messianic dawn has appeared, that the Kingdom is already here in the Person of Jesus.

The parable of the Strong Man expresses the fact that only he who has bound "the strong man"—in this case, Satan—is prepared to become master of his house. This is the meaning of the temptation in the wilderness (4:1-11). Jesus can deliver men from the power of Satan because Satan has no power over him. Jesus has confronted him and conquered (see John 14:30).

The stake in the battle is such that no one may remain neutral; it is necessary to be on the one side or the other (vs. 30). He who does not acknowledge Jesus as the One sent from God is already against him. He has come to proclaim and accomplish the great final gathering together of the children of God. Those who do not unite with him contribute to the scattering of God's children, for the art of Satan is to separate and destroy. Once more the image is that of a flock, of a shepherd who collects his sheep from the wolves who have scattered them (Ezek. 34:2-6, 11-16; compare Matt. 7:15; 9:36; John 10:11-12).

Jesus put his questioners on guard against the only sin which is without forgiveness—the sin against the Holy Spirit (vss. 31-32). He affirms that all sins and blasphemies may be pardoned, save this one. What is the sin against the Holy Spirit? The Holy Spirit is the Presence of God in us—the testimony of himself which God makes in the deepest level of our inner selves. Woe to the one who knowingly and willfully resists this summons, this Holy Presence. It is the voice of God which he refuses or denies and thus reduces to silence. He, so to speak, kills the Presence of God in him (see Heb. 6:4-6). Jesus recognizes that one may speak against him out of ignorance, and this sin may be pardoned (see Acts 3:17). The way of repentance and faith remains open. And if the sin against the Holy Spirit is not pardoned "either in this age or in the age to come," the opposite is true also—there is hope "in this age" and "in the age to come" for those who will not have been acquainted with or recognized the Son of Man here below.

Jesus does not say that his questioners have committed the sin against the Holy Spirit, but he warns them with an exceptional gravity that they could be on the way to doing so. Verses 33-34 state his thought precisely. The lack of sincerity on the part of his accusers arises from the fact that they could not condemn his act—the healing of the demoniac—yet they still declared that this act is the good fruit of a bad tree. But the fruit reveals the nature of the tree (see 7:16-20; Luke 6:43-44). The Pharisees' words have revealed an evil heart within. They do not seek the truth; they seek only to dishonor him. Their speech is loaded with deadly poison ("brood of vipers!"; compare 3:7; 23:29-33). "For out of the abundance of the heart the mouth speaks" (vs. 34). Thus our words reveal the bedrock of our being—good or bad.

It is to be noted here that Jesus recognized that there are some "good" men and some "evil" men; not, certainly, in the absolute sense, for he well knows that God alone is "good" (Mark 10:18; Matt. 19:17), but in a relative sense. There are for Jesus some "just" men whose hearts are right and humble before God, and there are "unjust" men. And it is especially in their words that this justice or this injustice reveals itself. Jesus puts us sternly on guard against the spirit of condemnation, against "careless" words, for it is by them that God will judge us (vss. 36-37; compare Matt. 7:1-5; Rom. 14:12-13; James 3:1-12).

The Pharisees Demand Signs (12:38-45)

What the Pharisees ask is a "sign" which will prove that Jesus is truly the Messiah—some sensational miracle of the sort from which Jesus had forever turned away at the Temptation (see 4:5-7; 16:1). They want God to manifest himself. Jesus sees in this request only an evidence of the unbelief and wickedness of those who surround him. The term "adulterous" describes the infidelity of Israel; it is a classic term from the Old Testament which compares the love of God for the Elect People to the love of a fiancé or a husband (see Jer. 2:1-5, 32; Hosea 2:16-23; Ezek. 16). Those who reject this love will not know how to recognize God when he comes to them; Jesus will give them no other sign than "the sign of the prophet Jonah" (compare Luke 11:29-32).

This saying is mysterious. Luke's account recalls only that at the preaching of Jonah, Nineveh repented. The faith of the pagans confounds and judges the unbelief of the Jews. Matthew's account goes further. As Jonah has known a sort of resurrection from the dead, so the Son of Man must die and be raised. Jesus thus announces his sufferings and resurrection. What he is will be manifested in due time. Both, however, clearly affirm his Messiahship; for who could be greater than a prophet, or greater than the majestic King Solomon, if not the Messiah?

The Messiah has come and has not been recognized by his own people. The example of Nineveh (Jonah 3) and that of the Queen of Sheba (see I Kings 10:1-10) anticipate a time when the Gentile nations will surpass Israel in faith. At the last day the faith of the Ninevites and the Queen of the South will be a condemnation of those who have steeled themselves against the preaching of repentance and have failed to recognize in Jesus the wisdom of God.

The little parable of verses 43-45 is addressed to those who, because they have been delivered once, believe themselves to be secure. Surreptitiously, when they least expect it, the demon returns in force, accompanied by "seven other spirits more evil than himself." This warning is addressed in the first instance to Israel. It has known great deliverances in the past; but it has left the house "empty," it has not kept in touch with the living God. Its fall will be only the more terrible in the hour of testing which is going to come upon it like a bolt out of the blue. But this warning goes beyond Israel and is addressed to believers of every age. Wherever the house is left "empty," the demons hasten there (see I Peter 5:8-9).

Who Are My Mother and My Brothers? (12:46-50)

The anxiety manifested by Jesus' relatives seems to be directly related to the conflict which has just taken place between him and the religious authorities and which has put his life in danger. This relationship is more clearly indicated in Mark than in Matthew (see Mark 3:20-35). At first glance the response of Jesus to the concern of his family seems hard. What he demands of others (see 10:34-39) he demands of himself. No human bond may impede his mission. There is only one way to be a member of his "family"—to do the will of his Father who is in heaven. It is in this trait, and in no other, that he recognizes his own. But to those who do this willingly, to the obedient who have left all to follow him, he grants the magnificent favor of calling them his "brothers" (see 19:27-30).

It would be false, however, to conclude from such an episode that Jesus took lightly the ties of the flesh. Such an attitude would have been contrary to the total teaching of the Old Testament (see 15:3-6). Later, one of his last words was for his mother (John 19:25-27). His mother and brothers were present with the disciples in the Upper Room (Acts 1:14). His brother James became a pillar of the Church (Gal. 1:19; 2:9). Thus, the separation of the moment eventuated in an eternity of glory for his own.

Once more Jesus puts life in the presence of the absolute demand of God. The anxious concern of families and their refusal to face the last sacrifice for those whom they love has ruined more vocations than the opposition of adversaries.

Parables of the Kingdom (13:1-52)

This new series of discourses is introduced by Matthew in a very lively fashion. We see Jesus going "out of the house" (see Mark 2:1-2), seating himself in a boat, and teaching the crowds massed on the shore. And he speaks to them "in parables" (13:3; see 13:34-35).

Teaching in parables is not peculiar to Jesus. The rabbis practiced it. We have instances of it in the Old Testament (see II Sam. 12:1-7; Judges 9:7-15; Ezek. 17:22-24). A truth in the spiritual realm is suggested by means of a story or an image borrowed from the material world. A parable is an analogy, and in each instance the point of comparison must be grasped. It is the "point" of the parable. A parable is not to be made into an allegory, where each detail has a hidden meaning. A parable is a popular manner of expressing one's thoughts, and Jesus took his parables from everyday life. By this means he communicated "hidden" things (13:34-35). But only those who are open to the things of God grasp their true meaning. These are the truths which are revealed "to babes" but hidden "from the wise and under-

standing" (see 11:25) or those who believe themselves to be
such. A parable is a veiled manner of treating the realities of the
faith, "the secrets of the kingdom" (13:10-17). Perhaps it is the
opposition of which Jesus is the object that leads him to choose
this mode of speaking.

The Parable of the Sower and Its Explanation
(13:1-23; Mark 4:1-20)

Goethe mentions with some irony this sower who cast his seed
indiscriminately on the edge of the road, on stony ground, and
in the brambles. What intelligent farmer would act thus? But is
not this paradox intentional? The point of the parable lies precisely in the contrast between the quantity of grain lost and the
final abundance of the harvest.

The sower is none other than Jesus. And how numerous are
those who reject his word! But no amount of opposition can prevent the coming of the Kingdom of God or his word from bearing
incalculable fruit! The parable is a judgment on those who listen
without understanding (see 13:19), but a marvelous promise to
those who hear the word and understand it (see 13:23). It concludes with a solemn warning: "He who has ears, let him hear"
(13:9; compare the same injunction in 13:43). When Jesus uses
this formula it always indicates an important revelation, a decisive
choice.

The parable itself (vss. 3-9) is followed by two explanations,
one bearing on the mystery of the Kingdom (vss. 10-17), the
other on the parable itself (vss. 18-23).

Jesus' reply to the question of the disciples (vss. 10-11)
seems at first glance to be enigmatic. Does Jesus deliberately
speak in a way not to be understood? Exactly the contrary is said
further on (vss. 34-35). We have seen earlier, however, that a
parable is at the same time a simple way of speaking to those who
understand but a stone of stumbling for those who do not.

What are these secrets of the Kingdom which are revealed to
the disciples only? First and essentially, they involve the fact
that the Kingdom of God is secretly but effectively present in the
Person of Jesus. The epoch of the Messianic Age has begun! This
is thrown into relief by all the sayings and all the mighty works
which we have been recounting, as well as by certain precise declarations of Jesus himself (see particularly 11:27-30; 12:28,
41-42). But the mystery of the Kingdom consists also in the fact

that the coming of Jesus produces a distinction between those who receive the good news of the Kingdom and those who reject it. His coming becomes a judgment which we pronounce on ourselves. The one "who has" will receive an abundance. The one "who has not" will lose even what he has (vs. 12). This saying, in its paradoxical form, reminds us that the word of God is never without effect. It either brings fulfillment or it hardens.

The quotation from Isaiah indicates that the presence of Jesus, as was true of the preaching of the prophet, places Israel before a final decision. Now, as then, Israel shuts her ears to the call of God. She is deaf and blind. She will not acknowledge herself to be sick, and thus she refuses her healing. But there are some in Israel who see and hear. Blessed are they! For they live in a unique hour, the time of the coming of the Messiah, that coming which the prophets and all the "righteous men" of the Old Testament had awaited through the centuries.

The unbelief of a large number is, in a way, to be expected in a world separated from God. It is a divine miracle that there are those who have seen and believed! It is a miracle that all the opposition of the world cannot prevent his Kingdom from coming or his harvest from being superabundant! This is both a warning and a promise for preachers and missionaries in every age.

The explanation of the parable of the Sower, as it is given in verses 18-23, makes clear the point on which the similitude turns: the seed is nothing other than the word of God, received by some, rejected by others. But it must be acknowledged that this explanation weakens rather than clarifies the mystery of the Kingdom spoken of above. It has a very practical import and does not throw into relief with equal force the central thought of the parable itself. Perhaps it is necessary to see here a homiletical commentary, an echo of the apostolic preaching. The warning is addressed to hearers in every age. It is already detached from the historic crisis which is the backdrop of this parable and of those which follow (vss. 10-17). In this case the passage merely prolongs the line of Jesus' thought by generalizing its meaning. In any case, it brings to each one of us an important message on the manner of our *hearing*.

There is a superficial way of reading the Bible and of participating in worship. The Word is read or heard, but it is not "understood." We do not receive inwardly all of its demand and its promise. It does not become within us a ferment of life (see 7:

21-27; 12:50). Also, the Devil is quick to obliterate the Word. We may have received it with enthusiasm, but it takes only one trial to shake our faith. That which comes upon us "on account of the word" leads us to fall away. Or, again, the daily "cares" of life "choke" the word, drown it in a whirlpool of activity. Thus we fail to bring forth the marvelous harvest promised to him who "hears the word and understands it."

The Tares, Mustard Seed, and Leaven (13:24-43)

The parable of the Tares, recorded only by Matthew (vss. 24-30), is separated from its explanation by two other short parables, the Mustard Seed (vss. 31-32; see Mark 4:30-32; Luke 13:18-19) and the Leaven (vs. 33; see Luke 13:20-21). Verses 34-35 serve as a sort of conclusion to this first collection of parables. The explanation of the Tares is given to his disciples in private by Jesus (vss. 36-43).

In the parable of the Tares, again seed is sown in a field. The new element, however, is the role of the "enemy" who also sows, secretly, during the night. The servants are astonished at the appearance of the tares and propose pulling them up. The householder denies their proposal for fear of uprooting the wheat. The separation will be made at the harvest.

Here again we are in the presence of a deliberate paradox. Can we imagine anyone, even an enemy, sowing bad seed in a neighbor's field? Nevertheless, such is the situation of the world: God is the legitimate owner, who has sowed the seed of his Word in the world. But another is there, the Adversary, Satan, who surreptitiously labors to destroy his work. Wherever the Spirit of God is at work with power, Satan also arrives in force! The Jews expected an immediate judgment at the Messianic Age; they thought that the Messiah would form around him the community of the "pure." (The Dead Sea Scrolls indicate that the Qumran sect tried to build such a community, separated from the world.) Now Jesus is here and the Evil One continues his work. Even among the Twelve there will be a traitor. The question, Why? was posed in the minds of the disciples. The Gospels do not hide from us the disciples' impatience with this different sort of judgment (see Luke 9:54-55), with this Kingdom which did not come quickly enough for their liking.

The "point" of the parable is precisely this mixture of wheat and tares, of good and evil, of good people and bad people, which

will exist "until the harvest," that is, to the end of the age (13:40).
Men are not permitted to prejudge the Last Judgment. We are
here confronted with the mystery of the patience of God.

The explanation of the parable in verses 36-43 states precisely its Messianic meaning, while it transposes its terms. The
enemy is the Devil. The seed consists, on the one hand, of "the
sons of the kingdom" and, on the other hand, of "the sons of the
evil one." When the last hour comes, the Son of Man, through
his angels, will cleanse his Kingdom of all impure elements. The
description of the fiery furnace where "men will weep and gnash
their teeth" is characteristic of Matthew (13:42, 50; 22:13; 24:51;
25:30) and is found only once elsewhere (Luke 13:28). One may
question whether this is not a stereotyped formula which is a
favorite of the editor. The point of the parable is not so much
the prohibition of judging before the time as it is the fear which
the Last Judgment should inspire. At the same time, however, the
essential warning remains the same: only the Last Judgment will
definitively reveal to *whom* we belong, and it will be either a judgment of death or a marvelous fullness of life—"the righteous will
shine like the sun in the kingdom of their Father" (vs. 43). It is
impossible to be sure how much of this interpretation is the actual
word of Jesus and how much is the commentary or preaching of the
Early Church; but this takes away nothing from the importance
of the message.

The parable of the Mustard Seed (vss. 31-32) stresses the
contrast between the smallness of the seed and the greatness of
the tree (compare Mark 4:30-32). The prophets sometimes described the kingdoms of the world under the form of a tree which
extended its branches over the whole earth (Ezek. 31:3-9; Dan.
4:11-12). Jesus applied this image to the Kingdom which he had
come to inaugurate. How humble and hidden its beginnings, but
how great the promise which it contains!

The parable of the Leaven likewise stresses the contrast between the end and the means (vs. 31; compare Luke 13:20-21).
Three measures of meal correspond to about forty pounds of
bread. Only a very little leaven is sufficient to make all this dough
rise!

The Treasure, the Pearl, and the Net (13:44-52)

The themes of the parables of the Treasure and of the Pearl
are the same: in both cases we are confronted with a man who dis-

covers something so precious that he is ready to sell all he has
to acquire it. The only difference between the two stories rests
in the fact that in the first case the man finds the treasure without having to look for it and hides it carefully until he is able
to acquire it, while in the second case the merchant is searching
for pearls and his search is rewarded.

The first thing which these parables tell us is that the proclamation of the Kingdom of God is good news. This note of joy
remains dominant in the message of Jesus through all opposition
and all defeat. In this his preaching is in strong contrast to that
of John the Baptist. His coming evokes the joy of a wedding (9:
14-15), the joy of a feast (11:16-19). Jesus both radiates and
communicates this joy. To know him is to know joy, the peace
of pardon, the freedom of the children of God. And this is the
joy that nothing can take away (see John 15:9-11; 16:22). Whoever catches a glimpse of such a gift is ready to leave all to receive
it. The word "renounce" has little meaning for him inasmuch as
he has only one desire! (see 6:19-21). To preach the gospel is
to reveal a *treasure*.

The parable of the Net allies itself with that of the Tares. The
fishermen draw out of the sea fish of all kinds; later they will
seat themselves on the shore and throw away what is bad. In this
Jesus evokes a familiar scene. The disciples have been compared
by him to "fishers of men" (4:19). The community which they
gather is a mixture of good and bad. The separation will take
place only at the Last Judgment. Here again it is the angels who
have charge of doing the sorting (compare 13:41-42).

"Have you understood all this?" This question addressed to
the disciples is addressed to us also. Have we understood? Have
we found the pearl which is worth more than all the treasures of
the world? Have we made our choice?

The meaning of the saying concerning the scribes (vs. 52) and
its link with what goes before is not absolutely clear. The reference is to scribes "trained for the kingdom of heaven." The saying is therefore addressed to the disciples, to all those who have
received the instruction of Jesus. They accumulate a treasure
where the old is mixed with the new. What are these old and new
things? They are presumably the revelations of the Old Testament, from which Jesus draws inspiration and whose authority
he upholds, and the extraordinary newness which lies in the coming of the Kingdom in his Person.

New Conflicts and New Miracles (13:53—16:12)

This series of accounts, the progress of which Matthew borrows from Mark (compare Mark 6:1-6; 6:14—8:21), unfolds without any great visible unity. It illustrates the preceding discourses—an ever-deepening chasm develops between the unbelief of some and the faith of others. We are apprised that the destiny reserved for prophets is rejection and martyrdom. We are thus slowly prepared for the confession of the disciples and the announcement of the Passion.

The Destiny of Prophets (13:53-58; see Mark 6:1-6)

It is not without reason that Matthew, following Mark, relates consecutively the rejection of Jesus by his home town and the beheading of John the Baptist. A common lesson is bound up in these two stories: the world does not tolerate prophets, for the mission of the prophet is to labor for the truth, to unmask falsehood (see 5:11-12; 23:29-31).

All three Synoptic Gospels note that the villagers of Nazareth were astonished. The reputation of Jesus had reached them, and his preaching had made an impression on them. They admitted that he had done great miracles in Capernaum (Luke 4:23). How was he able to do all this? We know his family! They are insignificant people! Certainly, everybody in the village is in expectation; but *it is the expectation of curiosity, not that of faith.* And Jesus never satisfies this sort of expectation. According to the Gospel by Luke, he abruptly unmasks the unbelief of his hearers, and this is sufficient to turn them against him (Luke 4:25-28). Mark and Matthew simply declare without explanation that the people "took offense" at Jesus. Because they believed that they knew him, with a completely human knowledge, they did not recognize in him the messenger of God, the bringer of salvation. "And he did not do many mighty works there, because of their unbelief." The Kingdom of God does not open up its mystery to the curious but to the poor, to those who thirst after righteousness (see 5:3-8). Nazareth is not ready to receive it. And Jesus declares that a prophet is of no account in his own country. Jesus knew, among other sufferings, the pain of being a stranger among his own people.

The Death of John the Baptist (14:1-12; see Mark 6:14-29).

The story of the beheading of John the Baptist lays bare the weakness, the cruelty, and the superstitious fears of that ill-fated person, King Herod. He would perhaps have spared the life of the prophet, either from political considerations (14:4) or from fear (Mark 6:20), but the seductiveness of a girl and an oath likely pronounced while drunk were sufficient to bring about the murder.

And now there arises another prophet, whose reputation reaches the palace (vs. 1). Herod trembles. Could this be John the Baptist alive again? Fear produced by a troubled conscience inevitably was to be transposed into hatred. Herod was perhaps the only person whom Jesus had openly scorned (see Luke 13: 31-33; 23:9).

The Miracle of the Loaves and the Fish (14:13-21; see Matt. 15:32-38; Mark 6:35-44; 8:1-9; Luke 9:10-17; John 6:1-14)

At the news of the death of John the Baptist, Jesus withdrew for a time to a lonely place, on the other side of the lake. This territory offered greater security, since it was under the jurisdiction of the Tetrarch Philip. The Gospel writers point us to several such retreats of Jesus. He avoided open conflict until the hour appointed by the Father had come. Soon he will announce that this hour is near.

The crowds followed Jesus "on foot"; that is, they went around the lake to rejoin him. They listened to his teaching with such eagerness that evening came before any provision had been made for food. The disciples grew uneasy. Jesus replied to them: "You give them something to eat."

The story of the multiplication of the loaves is reproduced six times in the four Gospels. It had assumed, therefore, a particular importance in the Gospel tradition. What is its significance? This is the true question. For the raw fact, the "how" of this multiplication of bread, always escapes us, and we are obliged to receive the story just as the tradition has transmitted it to us.

The story underlines first the concern of Jesus for the bodily needs of men. Jesus is disturbed by the hunger of this crowd and commands his disciples to feed them. And this remains true for all times. The compassion of Jesus (vs. 14) includes the whole man. He had refused to perform a miracle of bread for himself (4:3), but he remains all-powerful to feed the hungry whom God has put in his way, and he desires that the faith of his disciples should achieve the same result, no matter how meager their means! This message is very important in today's world where the contrast is more acute than ever between "the haves" and "the have nots."

In the second place, this act points to scriptural precedents. Had not Moses, at God's order, fed Israel in the wilderness? (Exod. 16). Had not Elisha fed a hundred men with "twenty loaves of barley" and a few ears of grain? (II Kings 4:42-44). Here is One greater than Moses and Elisha.

The essential point of the story, however, is the Messianic meaning which it conveys. In New Testament times the coming Kingdom was described under the form of a banquet (see 8:11). Prior to this, in the Old Israel the Covenant was sealed by a meal (see Gen. 14:18; Exod. 24:9-11). Jesus is shown opening the meal by giving thanks (vs. 19). This brotherly love feast anticipates the Lord's Supper, and beyond that Supper the great gathering of the children of God at the banquet of the Kingdom. It is this meaning which John gives to this event (John 6).

Will not the permanent miracle of the Church, which is the fruit of prayer and of love, be the nourishing of the crowds with "five loaves and . . . two fish"? Will not the mystery of God in every age be the astonishing disproportion between our human means and the unlimited power of his grace?

Peter Walking on the Water
(14:22-36; compare Mark 6:45-56; John 6:15-21; Matt. 8:23-27)

Jesus withdrew from his disciples "by himself to pray" (vss. 22-23). Do we have a clear idea of how rare solitude was at this point in the life of Jesus? He found it only in the night; and in order to find it he had to flee the conditions resulting from tiny lodging quarters, that cruel lack of privacy imposed on the poor. To speak with his Father he had to go alone out into the fields by night.

We have three accounts of the nighttime crossing which followed the multiplication of the loaves (Matt. 14:22-33; Mark 6:45-52; John 6:15-21). These are three traditions of the same event. All three point out the difficulty of the crossing and the sudden appearance of Jesus. They all indicate that the disciples did not recognize Jesus at first, and that he came toward them "walking on the sea." Matthew alone relates that Peter asked to go to meet the Lord; he walked on the water, but he was seized with fear and immediately began to sink and to cry for help. Jesus said to him, "O man of little faith, why did you doubt?" And all those in the boat prostrated themselves before the Lord, saying, "Truly you are the Son of God." The mystery of this appearance of Jesus calls to mind the post-Resurrection appearance (see John 21). The disciples' confession of faith anticipates that which will be made a little later (Matt. 16:16). It is permissible to raise the question whether we do not have here a certain development of the tradition in which the memory of the Risen One blends with that of the earthly ministry of Jesus. But the story as it has come to us is the bearer of a double message: (1) Jesus is Lord of the elements. He is clothed with the very power of God. He is not only the teacher whom they follow but also the Son before whom they prostrate themselves. (2) The faith which looks to Jesus only and obeys his word dares and can do anything. But the faith which begins to doubt "sinks," and runs the risk of foundering if the merciful hand of the Lord were not extended to save. Through the impulsive character of Peter, this story describes our own faith with its starts and failures.

The chapter concludes with one of those summaries of which the writer is fond and in which he likes to frame his stories. It shows us Jesus disembarking once more on the Galilean shore and the crowds flocking toward him.

A Debate Over What Is "Pure" and "Impure"
(15:1-20; see Mark 7:1-23)

The Pharisees and scribes who question Jesus come "from Jerusalem." Doubtless they have been charged with keeping an eye on these Galileans whose piety was considered not strict enough, and particularly on this new rabbi who had too much to say. The attack was based on the fact that the disciples did not wash their hands before meals. Jesus counterattacked by posing another question, a device very similar to rabbinic methods of argument. To "tradition" he opposed "the commandment of God."

"Tradition," or "the tradition of the elders," is a standard term to designate the oral tradition which little by little was created as a kind of jurisprudence for the purpose of explaining and adapting the Mosaic Law to the needs of the time. In this fashion some very strict ritual prescriptions were developed with regard to the ablutions which should precede eating in order to avoid all ceremonial defilement (see Mark 7:3-4). In his reply Jesus alluded to another tradition: one could declare "Corban"—that is, devoted to God—the goods which ought to have been used to aid his parents. This was a vow which discharged him who pronounced it from family obligations, yet did not deprive him of the use of his goods! Jesus set over against such traditions the Word of God—the fifth commandment of the Decalogue (Exod. 20:12) and the severe judgment which follows in Exodus 21:17. He also applied to his questioners a word of Isaiah (Isa. 29:13): they honor God in words but not in heart. Verses 10-11 take up again the heart of the question posed by the scribes. It is not foods which defile a man but that which "comes out of the mouth"—evil words.

The disciples inform Jesus of the "scandal" which his words provoked (vs. 12). The word means literally "something which causes to stumble." But Jesus is not troubled. God knows his own, and all that he has not planted will be uprooted. His will be the sorting, his the harvest! "Let them alone." The Pharisees are "blind." They do not discern the signs of the coming Kingdom. That is why they "fall" and involve others in their ruin.

The parable of verse 11 seems clear; nevertheless, the disciples ask for an explanation (vss. 15-20; compare Matt. 13:10-16). Could their desire for an explanation be rooted in the manner in which Jesus rejects established traditions, such as those concerning ritual ablutions? There is something so revolutionary in his attitude that their minds have difficulty in following him. Jesus explains that nothing exterior can defile a man, but only that which comes "out of the heart." Verse 19 recalls the Ten Commandments. Here, as in the Sermon on the Mount, Jesus goes behind the act to the thought which has prompted it (5:21-48). To all exterior practices he sets in opposition the conversion of the heart which is the mark of the New Age (see Jer. 31:33). Here again, it is because Jesus inaugurates the New Age that he can free his own from bondage to tradition. Religious conformity can be only a mask thrown over the wickedness of the heart.

The Faith of a Gentile (15:21-28)

There is perhaps a deliberate contrast here between this story and the preceding one, between the unbelief of the "officials" of Israel and the humble faith of this Gentile. Matthew recounts in a singularly vivid but much more brutal fashion than Mark (see Mark 7:24-30) the impatience of the disciples and the harshness of Jesus' replies. Jesus has once more withdrawn to a distance from the Galilean crowds. He has crossed the Syrian frontier, no doubt to search for a little bit of silence and calm with his disciples.

The saying of verse 24, "I was sent only to the lost sheep of the house of Israel," brings to mind a similar word spoken at the time of the sending of the Twelve on their mission (10:5-6). We have seen in that connection that it did not involve any racial exclusivism but was solely a question of priority in time. In the Messianic Age the gathering of Israel must precede and prepare for the gathering of the nations. It is to the children of the election and the promise that the grace of God must first be offered, because of the vocation which is theirs and the responsibility which it entails. But here the prayer of the woman is made entreatingly. It is the true cry of faith: "Lord, help me." Jesus still withstands the request. Or can it be that he wishes to test this newborn faith? "It is not fair to take the children's bread . . ." The woman accepts this priority of the "children"; she only asks for "the crumbs." Her humility matches that of the centurion, "I am not worthy" (8:8). That Gentile man and this Gentile woman count upon the liberating word as pure grace with no justification whatever. It is in this that their faith is "great." Are they not given to Jesus by the Father as the first fruits of the future harvest?

Various Healings and the Second Miracle of Loaves (15:29-39)

We have seen that Matthew likes to frame his particular stories in more general descriptions designed to make the abundance of Jesus' activity and his success with the crowds stand out (see 14: 34-36; also 4:23-25; 9:35). The description in verses 30-31 recalls Isaiah 35:5-6. The crowds were in admiration and "glorified the God of Israel." They recognized the hand of the Living God in Jesus' activity, and to him their praises went forth (see 5:16).

These healings take place in "the hills." Jesus is at a distance from the villages, perhaps with a desire to flee publicity. But "the hills" are for the evangelists a reminder of Sinai. It is on a mountain that God traditionally reveals his presence and his power; it is there that he speaks and acts (see 5:1; 14:23; 15:29; 17:1-2; Mark 3:13).

The story in verses 32-39 reminds us in detail, almost to the exact figures, of the story in 14:15-21. Jesus is moved with "compassion" for this crowd which has just passed "three days" without anything "to eat," and he feeds them. The question naturally arises whether we do not have here a slightly different version of the same event. The story confronts us at one and the same time with an act of human compassion and a Messianic act wherein the great power of the Lord is revealed (see Mark 8:1-9).

The Pharisees Request a Sign (16:1-12; see Mark 8:11-21)

The request of the Pharisees calls to mind the same form in 12:38; but this time the Sadducees—that is, the priests—are also mentioned. "A sign from heaven" is to be understood as some clear proof which Jesus might give of his Messiahship. Jesus replies with an image. They know well how to discern what the weather is going to be by the color of the sky and the clouds. But they cannot discern "the signs of the times." Jesus obviously refers to the Messianic time which he announces and incarnates in his own Person. The expression "adulterous generation" means what the Old Testament meant by this term—a generation which has turned away from the living God and betrayed his love. For such a generation all "signs" would be in vain. For "the sign of Jonah" see 12:38-41.

Verses 5-12 confront us with a new misunderstanding on the part of the disciples. They often are decidedly "without understanding" (see 15:16). Let us admire the honesty with which the Gospel writers depict this slowness in understanding the true thought of Jesus, these frequent blunders. What patience is necessary on the part of their Master! And it is into their hands that he delivers his flock! There is here both encouragement and consolation for Christians in every age.

In this particular case, Jesus speaks figuratively; but the disciples, who have in their minds the fact that they had forgotten to buy bread, take his saying literally. They are more preoccupied with their immediate and material needs than with the hostility which has once more manifested itself against their teacher. The thread of their thoughts is other than that of Jesus; this is why there is no meeting of minds. Their anxiety about bread calls in question the faithfulness of God of which they have just had evidence.

What did Jesus wish to say by the expression "the leaven of

the Pharisees and Sadducees"? In Jewish tradition leaven is an impure ferment; it is bread without leaven which is pure (Lev. 2:11; compare I Cor. 5:7-8). The teaching of the Pharisees and the Sadducees is compared to the bad ferment which penetrates the entire batch of dough; these teachers deceive the people about what the true righteousness of God is (see 5:20). They substitute the commandments of men, human securities, for that obedience which is the authentic tradition of Israel. By subtle arguments they seek to undermine the authority of Jesus and to sow doubt among those who hear him. And already, they secretly plan to destroy him.

The Apostolic Church counted some Pharisees among its members, and certain others were fair-dealing opponents (see Acts 5: 33-39); but it was also from the Pharisees that the Church ran up against the most systematic opposition. Jesus was already preparing his disciples for these future struggles.

THE WAY TO THE PASSION
Matthew 16:13—23:39

Who Is Jesus? (16:13—17:27)

The Confession of Peter (16:13-20; Mark 8:27-30; Luke 9:18-21)

We come here to a crucial moment in the ministry of Jesus, when he confronts his disciples with the decisive question: "Who do you say that I am?" The importance of the conversation which is about to take place is underlined by the fact that Jesus takes the disciples outside Galilean territory, far from the crowds, far also from the control of the suspicious Herod, in the direction of Caesarea Philippi.

Jesus poses two distinct questions: "Who do *men* say . . .?" and "Who do *you* say . . .?" Matthew has indicated several times that the crowds were "astonished"; they "marveled" both at the teaching of Jesus and at his miracles. Everybody is asking who this man is, this one who calls himself "the Son of man." Some think that he is John the Baptist brought to life again (see 14:1-2); others that he is Elijah—Elijah in his day had done some great miracles and his return at the end of the age was expected (see Mal. 4:5); others that he is Jeremiah, doubtless because of the vigor with which Jeremiah had denounced the religion of his time. They discussed at length. Men have not ceased to discuss who Jesus is for twenty centuries, and the greater part of mankind remains just there. It is a long way from admiration to commitment.

The disciples have become involved. They have lived with their Master day after day; they have believed his promises; they have obeyed his call. They have been confronted with the mystery of his Person. God has revealed to them the hidden meaning of his words (11:27; 13:11). And now, the hour is come when Jesus calls them to confess their faith: "You are the Christ, the Son of the living God."

The terms which Matthew places in the mouth of Simon Peter are more explicit than those in Mark's and Luke's accounts (see Mark 8:29; Luke 9:20). But they have the same meaning, and they reflect an Old Testament mode of speech. God called his Anointed his "son" (see Ps. 2:2-7); God is frequently called "the living God." The high priest, in the trial of Jesus, used the same terms (26:63). These are the standard Messianic expressions.

The declaration of Jesus which follows (vss. 17-19) is found only in the Gospel by Matthew, and people are sometimes astonished that Jesus could declare an apostle "blessed" to whom, a few moments later, he will say, "Get behind me, Satan!" They are also astonished at the unique role here given to Peter. No objections urged against this text seem convincing.

To recognize in Jesus no longer merely a prophet but *the Son of God* is given only to faith; and this faith can only be a gift of God. Has Jesus not said that "no one knows the Son except the Father"? (11:27). Paul declares: "No one can say 'Jesus is Lord' except by the Holy Spirit" (I Cor. 12:3). The entire Apostolic Church recognized that the divinity of Jesus Christ is a mystery of faith, inaccessible to human wisdom alone, which is otherwise called, according to a classic Hebrew expression, "flesh and blood"—the natural man. When Simon confesses his faith, it is God himself speaking through his mouth. Great grace is given to him, and Jesus proclaims him "blessed." Jesus calls him by his Aramaic name, "Simon Bar-Jona" (son of Jona), and gives him a new name, "Peter" (or Cephas), which means *rock* (see I Cor. 1:12; Gal. 2:9). The play on words in verse 18 indicates the Aramaic origin of the passage. The new name contains a promise. "Simon," the fluctuating, impulsive disciple, will, by the grace of God, be the "rock" on which God will build the new community.

Jesus knows Peter's weakness but entrusts his brothers to him (see Luke 22:31-34). The testimony of the Acts shows that Peter is the recognized leader of the Apostolic Church, at least at its beginning (Acts 1:15; 2:14; 3:12; 4:8; see I Cor. 15:5; Gal. 1:18; 2:7). He is the first confessor of the faith which will later become the faith of the whole Church.

Here, for the first time, we meet with the term "church" on the lips of Jesus. It appears only twice in the entire Gospel by Matthew (see 18:17), never in the others. Some have concluded that this word was added by the evangelist. But it is an idea which arises naturally out of the entire Gospel. Jesus has intended to gather around him the faithful "remnant" and to lay the foundations of a new community. The choice of the Twelve gives proof of this. The Greek term for "church" used by Matthew signifies "assembly" and was at that time employed in the Greek translation of the Old Testament to designate the assembly of believers. Jesus spoke Aramaic and it is impossible to know exactly what term he employed to designate the nascent community. At the time when the evangelist edited his Gospel, the current term to designate this community was "the church."

Jesus made the promise to his Church that "the gates of Hades shall not prevail against it" (vs. 18, margin). By Hades, Jewish tradition understood the abode of the dead conceived as a place closed forever for those who entered it. Jesus here proclaims his *victory over death*. The scribes were thought of as retaining "the keys" of the Kingdom of God, but they had shut off access to it for men (Matt. 23:13; Luke 11:52). Jesus opens it and gives to his Church the power to open it for those who will receive his word. This word has the power of "loosing" men from the bonds of sin and of death. But it is the condemnation of those who reject it.

Jesus enjoins his disciples to tell no one that he is the Christ (vs. 20; see Mark 8:30). Here we are confronted with what has been called "the Messianic secret." The hour has not come to reveal his identity: on the one hand, because his ministry is not yet completed and the public confession of his Messiahship would lead to the sentence of death (see 26:62-66); on the other hand, because his nature as "Messiah" can lead to grave misunderstandings. The rest of his conversation with his disciples gives evidence of this.

The Announcement of Suffering
(16:21-28; Mark 8:31—9:1; Luke 9:22-27)

Jesus chooses this moment to speak to the disciples about the sufferings which await him. He tells them openly that the leaders of his people are going to put him to death. The disciples understand only that, and not the announcement of his resurrection which follows—and they are indignant. Certainly the hostility to which Jesus was exposed would give them a presentiment that he would, like the prophets, meet the fate of the prophets (see Luke 13:33). But how could the Messiah, the Son of God, be at the mercy of men? God, at the last moment, will manifest his power! Such is the meaning of Peter's protest. The idea of a suffering Messiah, of a Messiah put to death, is a scandal both for Peter's heart and for his mind. No! God will not permit that! But Jesus recognizes, in the voice of this disciple and friend, the voice of the Tempter who earlier, in the wilderness, had attempted to divert him from naked obedience to the single will of God and to lure him into easier paths. Jesus' reply is severe: "Get behind me, Satan!" Thus, the same man may be, in the interval of a few moments, the mouthpiece of God and the mouthpiece of Satan!

The force of this reply reveals the inner struggle Jesus is going through. Just because he is truly God and truly man, he measures, as no one else can, the horror of treachery, of abandonment, and of death. But he knows also that this death, beyond all secondary and human causes, is inscribed in the eternal plan of God: "he *must* . . . suffer." How hidden and mysterious are the thoughts of God! Are we astonished that Peter should be perplexed? Have we also not sometimes heard the reassuring voice of a friend who tries to divert us from a difficult duty: "Surely God does not demand that!" How we could wish that he were right!

The disciples' lack of understanding makes the way of the Passion a strange, radically solitary way for Jesus. The disciples never cease to hope for a divine intervention. Jesus goes toward the Cross, they toward glory. In order that they might understand this mystery of the Servant crucified for the salvation of men, a new revelation of God will be necessary, even the Resurrection and the descent of the Holy Spirit. But Jesus informs them now that this way of the Cross is not only his; it is also theirs (vss. 24-28). Men will reject them as they have rejected him. The words of verses 24-25 should be taken literally in the first instance: Jesus is preparing his Apostles for the possibility of martyrdom. They have a secondary meaning which is spiritual: to live life for God it is necessary to consent to the death of the self.

The natural man within us loves himself. He has a thirst for being loved, for being esteemed by man, for playing a part, for success. The life which Jesus proposes for us is a life given up, whose center and motive force are no longer our ego and its ambitions, but God and his will for the salvation of all men. It is a new mode of existence, it is true life. Everything else passes away and is only vanity. "For what will it profit a man, if he gains the whole world and forfeits his life?"

Under a familiar paradoxical form—to save one's life is to lose it, to lose one's life is to save it—Jesus confronts all those who desire to follow him with the final question, the question of the meaning of their existence: For whom, for what, do you live? This saying must have left a deep mark on the first disciples, for it is cited several times (see Matt. 10:38-39, and parallels).

To those who will follow him on the way of sacrifice, Jesus opens the prospect of an eternity of glory (vs. 27). The Cross is not God's last word. The Son of Man will return, and then he will be resplendent with all the glory of the Father. He will come "with his angels" as King and as Judge.

Verse 28 may be understood to refer to a coming in the near future. Did Jesus believe his return to be imminent? This saying and some other words which we have seen earlier (10:23) seem to indicate that he did. But he is very guarded about specifying times and seasons (see 24:36). It is not the time of his return that is important but the assurance of this last accomplishment. The Son of Man, the crucified, is the one to whom God has entrusted the judgment of the world, and those who have confessed him and followed him in his humiliation will know him in all the brightness of his glory.

The Transfiguration (17:1-13; Mark 9:2-13; Luke 9:28-36)

The Transfiguration scene is like an announcement or foreshadowing of the future glory just mentioned. Jesus takes the three disciples who were closest to him "up a high mountain apart." He appears to them resplendent with light as he will one day appear as the glorified Son of Man. What does the presence of Moses and Elijah signify? We have seen earlier that Jesus is considered in the Gospel as a new Moses; he is also the prophet of the New Age proclaiming the charter of the Kingdom of God. Moses had announced Jesus' coming (Deut. 18:15-19; see John 5:45-46; Luke 24:27). Elijah is the forerunner who is to prepare for the coming of the Messiah (Mal. 4:5-6). These two great figures by their presence confirm the Messianic mission of Jesus and the indissoluble bond which binds the New Covenant to the Old, the fulfillment to the promise. The Mount of the Transfiguration corresponds to Mount Sinai. It is there that God descends and reveals himself.

Peter, completely perplexed by this vision, would like to prolong it. But the hours spent on the mount remain here below as exceptional hours. It is necessary to redescend into the battle of life. A luminous cloud covered the appearances as it had covered Moses earlier at Sinai (Exod. 24:15). A voice rang out, as it had rung out at the hour of the Baptism (Matt. 3:17); for it is toward a new baptism, this time of blood, that Jesus advances in the obedience of faith (see Luke 12:49-50). The Father a second time acknowledges as his own this Son who has chosen the way of humiliation, the way of the Cross. It is in this unlimited self-giving that the Son reveals the Father; and the voice of the Father confirms this act of giving and hallows it.

The disciples, we are told, fall on their faces to the ground. The approach of God is always experienced in the Bible as something very majestic, very terrible. The fear which God's presence brings to birth is none other than the dread of a sinful man before the Holy God (see, for example, Isa. 6:1-5; Luke 5:8-10; Rev. 1:17). And the response is also the same: "Fear not"; "Have no fear." To him who knows and acknowledges himself to be unworthy God always shows his merciful face. The vision disappears, and Jesus alone is there, just as the Apostles have seen him and known him all along.

Once more Jesus enjoins silence; the revelation which has just been given to fortify their faith must not be communicated until later. The disciples immediately inquire about the coming of Elijah. Jesus reveals to them that "Elijah has already come"; but men have not recognized him and they "did to him whatever they pleased." It will be the same with the Son of Man. Men will do to him whatever they please. But without knowing it they will accomplish the purpose of One greater than they. For the purpose of God is achieved by and in spite of men.

The Healing of the Epileptic Boy
(17:14-23; Mark 9:14-29; Luke 9:37-42)

In this incident the Apostles fall from the loftiest summits to the hard realities of daily life. Is it not often so with us? A man throws himself at Jesus' feet and implores his help for his son. His disciples have not been able to cure him! Jesus has a singularly severe word which applies both to his disciples and to ourselves. He accuses his contemporaries of being a "faithless and perverse generation." He does not hide the fact that he has difficulty in enduring them. The impotence of the disciples shows how little is their faith! What is faith, for Jesus? It is not a simple creedal belief; it is the assurance that everything is possible to God, the assurance that he gives what he promises and what he ordains. Faith is a power which "moves mountains." To remove mountains is to know that there is no burden so heavy that God cannot help us to carry it, no problem so insoluble that he cannot resolve it. If Jesus accused his first disciples of unbelief, what does he think of us today? What patience must he have to continue to tolerate us?

The following saying (vss. 22-23) is a further reference to Jesus' approaching sufferings and the Resurrection which will follow them. But the disciples do not seem to grasp the announcement of the Resurrection; they only lay hold of the approaching departure of their Master and they are sad.

The Payment of the Temple Tax (17:24-27)

The annual tax which the Jews paid into the Temple was a half-shekel (worth about thirty-three cents). The essential point of the story is not the miracle but the remark of Jesus. He would have the right, inasmuch as he was the Son of God, to be exempt from the tax; and he extended this right to his disciples, for they also had access, through him, to the freedom of the sons of God. If Jesus pays the tax it is by condescension, in order not to "scandalize" those who have not yet understood the mystery of his coming, for he is free in regard to the Law. The miracle which follows indicates that God himself provides for all his needs.

The New Community (18:1-35)

Great and Small in the Kingdom (18:1-14; Mark 9:33-49)

The Gospel by Mark sketches a very vivid picture of this episode, showing the disciples wholly occupied with the question of their own greatness and Jesus taking a little child in his arms and giving them an example. These details are lacking in Matthew. He includes only the question posed here by the disciples themselves, and the reply of Jesus.

What is it to "become like children"? In what sense is a little child "humble"? The little child *knows himself to be small*. He does not pretend to be anything other than he is. He makes himself neither smaller nor greater than he is. Is that not true humility? One who sees himself in the light of his Father who is in heaven knows himself to be small. He is ready to take the lowest place in the Kingdom with joyous gratitude (see Mark 10:15).

To receive a little child in the name of Jesus, for the love of Jesus, is to receive Jesus himself. Jesus here stresses how precious the life of a child is in the eyes of God: to soil or to defile the soul of a child, or to disturb his faith, is a thing so serious that it would be better for a man to be put to death rather than to commit such a crime.

The saying of Jesus about scandals ("temptations," vs. 7) is a declaration: in this lost world which is a prey to sin, occasions of downfall abound. But woe to the one who causes another to fall! It would be better to remove a limb than to succumb to this temptation; this means to discern that within us which is secretly a party to this temptation and to consent to the necessary amputations (vss. 8-9; compare the same words, Matt. 5:29-30). The image employed by Jesus is radical, for to be deprived of a limb is a costly sacrifice which leaves us mutilated. But that is better than to allow gangrene to set in and corrupt the entire body. Hence, some privations or separations may be imperative for us even in relation to things which are quite legitimate in themselves but which expose us to danger. Each one must determine for himself the disciplines which are necessary to the health of his body and his spirit (see I Cor. 9:24-27).

The "little ones" in verses 10-14 are doubtless, in the first instance, children (see 18:1-6; 19:13-15), but the term includes

those who resemble children—the poor, the humble in heart.
"Little ones" often means merely "disciples."

In biblical tradition the angels are heavenly creatures which
God sends to men as his servants and messengers. As heavenly
counterparts they watch over believers. Those whom Jesus here
calls "little ones" are the children of the Kingdom; their "angels"
always gaze on the face of God.

The parable of the Lost Sheep (vss. 12-14) is given in more
elaborate form in the Gospel by Luke. It refers there to the lost
sheep of the house of Israel who are scorned by the Pharisees
(Luke 15:1-7). Here Matthew seems to be thinking more of the
little ones who are the weak members of the newborn community.
God is not willing that any of them should perish. The return of
a single one of these "little ones" who stray is a cause of great joy
for the keeper of the flock. To be sure, for Matthew as for Luke
this joy is felt "in heaven" (Luke 15:7), but it is also experienced
in the Church.

Of Pardon (18:15-35; compare Luke 17:3-4)

Here again, the thought concerns the new community established by Jesus. The question may be raised whether verses 15-17
go back to Jesus himself or whether they are the fruit of a later
development. In fact, the words "let him be to you as a Gentile
and a tax collector" seem to be at variance with the merciful attitude of Jesus precisely with regard to Gentiles and tax collectors
(see 9:10-13). The Church, living in a pagan environment, had
very early to impose certain disciplinary measures to safeguard
the purity of the gospel (see I Cor. 5). The passage here speaks
of "brothers," that is, men who have accepted the gospel. On this
account their conduct is more serious.

The brother is first to be reproved by the offended party alone
with all due discretion. His bad conduct is not to be publicized.
If he will not listen, then two or three witnesses are to confront
him (see Deut. 19:15). Finally, as a third step, he is to be brought
before the whole assembled community. To treat him as "a Gentile" means to cast him out of the fellowship of the Church. This
means concretely excommunication. To do this is to deliver him
again to the powers of evil from which the preaching of the
gospel had delivered him. Does he not thereby become anew the
object of evangelism?

Such is the meaning of verse 18, which we have encountered

before (16:19). But what is there said to Simon Peter is here spoken to the Christian community. The Word of God, of which the Church is the depository, has power to bind and to loose. It frees him who receives it; it casts back into slavery him who resists it.

Verses 19-20 contain a great and magnificent promise with regard to the prayer of believers: where two or three are united on "anything they ask" of God, they will obtain it, because it is to the Father of Jesus Christ and in the name of Jesus Christ that this prayer is made. The "name" in biblical language expresses the profound reality of a person. To speak or to act in the name of Jesus Christ is to invoke his presence and his power; it is to call upon that which he is, to conform the will to his. This is why Jesus can say that where two or three are met "in my name" he is present in the midst of them. This is also why their prayer is certain to be granted, for he himself inspires it and prays in them. He is their guarantor with his Father.

The Apostle Peter, once more the spokesman for his brothers, raises the question about pardon (vss. 21-22). Must one pardon seven times? Jesus replies, "Seventy times seven," which is a way of saying, *always*. The number recalls the ancient word of Lamech who avenged himself "seventy-sevenfold" (Gen. 4:24). To the absolute of vengeance is opposed the absolute of pardon.

Jesus illustrates his thought by telling a parable about an insolvent debtor for whom the creditor mercifully remitted his debt, but who, upon going out, refused all mercy to an unfortunate one who owed him a tiny sum. The contrast between the two sums and the two attitudes constitutes the point of the parable. The relationship is that of ten million dollars to twenty dollars! How could one to whom God has given his grace crush his brother? There is no comparison possible between the pardon of God and that which we grant to others, no matter how great the offense sustained. One who does not pardon his neighbor excludes himself by that from communion with God. Jesus several times returns to this thought. He who shuts out mercy shows thereby that he has understood nothing of the love of God, of the extraordinary pardon of which he himself is the object (see 5:7, 43-48; 6:12-15).

On the Way Toward Jerusalem (19:1—20:34)

Jesus leaves Galilee, this time for the south, and betakes himself to Judea. He crosses the Jordan and directs his steps toward Jerusalem through Perea, by way of Jericho. The crowds, Matthew tells us, continue to follow him.

The Question of Divorce (19:1-12; Mark 10:1-12)

The Pharisees brought up the problem of divorce to Jesus not so much to get light on it as to "test" him by entangling him in their casuistry. This question, in fact, was a subject of discussion among the diverse rabbinic schools: On what grounds was a man permitted to put away his wife? Certain ones considered it sufficient cause if she had burned a meal. Jesus did not enter into the game of his adversaries, but simply urged on them the law of creation as God himself had established it (Gen. 2:24). "What therefore God has joined together, let no man put asunder." But the Pharisees defend themselves by citing the Law of Moses (Deut. 24:1). Jesus replies that Moses had established this rule "for your hardness of heart." Legislation is obliged to take account of human weaknesses. In the days of Moses, as in our own, law can only put a certain bridle on the passions of men and put in order some situations which have become abnormal. But in the eyes of God the fault entirely remains. One single case of misconduct is here excepted, because in this case the break is already accomplished (see comment on Matt. 5:27-28, 31-32).

The disciples are alarmed at the strictness of Jesus. The obligation to consider marriage as an indissoluble bond, for life, seems to them to surpass the power of man (vs. 10). They have not grasped what the vocation of marriage is, the total giving of two persons to each other so that they are no longer two but one. They therefore raise the question of celibacy.

Jesus' reply is expressed in very enigmatic language, and he himself underlined the fact that only they understand this saying to whom understanding is given (vss. 11-12). There is a compulsory celibacy. But celibacy may be a vocation freely accepted for the purpose of an exclusive devotion to the service of God (see Jer. 16:1-2).

In the history of the Church, Roman Catholicism has exalted celibacy as a more perfect state. Protestantism has reacted by exalting marriage as being the normal vocation for all men and women. Jesus recognized both vocations as gifts of God without establishing the priority of one over the other. Each person is to follow, but follow to the end, with all the renunciations which that implies, the way to which he has been called.

Jesus Blesses Little Children
(19:13-15; Mark 10:13-16; Luke 18:15-17)

This brief scene is one of those on which Christian parents love to fix their attention: through these little ones from a Judean village, does Jesus not look on their own children and bless them? What a contrast there is between the attitude of Jesus and that of his disciples! For them, these people who press around the Master with their little ones in their arms are intruders. They interrupt some otherwise important and serious conversations! And was there not a little superstition in the desire that Jesus lay his hands on some babies for whom this gesture had no meaning? But Jesus sees things otherwise. He loves these little ones and declares that the Kingdom is for those who resemble them (see 18:1-6, 10). He places his hands on them in blessing.

The Problem of the Rich Young Man
(19:16-30; Mark 10:17-31; Luke 18:18-30)

The story of the rich young man greatly disturbed the disciples. It has not ceased to disturb Christians. This man is a devout Jew. He takes the commandments of the Law seriously. He desires to do what is "good." He is anxious to inherit eternal life. The Gospel by Mark tells us that "Jesus looking upon him loved him" (Mark 10:21). According to Mark, Jesus said to him: "You lack one thing"; according to Matthew, it is the young man himself who asks: "What do I still lack?" Jesus said to him: "If you would be perfect . . ." Confronted with the demand to sell what he possessed and to follow Jesus, the young man went away "sorrowful."

Jesus has not demanded of all his disciples that they abandon their goods. If he demands it here, it is without doubt because he has discerned between this man and the Kingdom a major obstacle—his possessions. Placed before the final decision, the young man does not have the courage to take the last step and "leave all" to follow Jesus. Mammon, the god of riches, gets the better of Jesus Christ in this man's decision (see 6:24).

To limit this episode to one individual case would, nevertheless, falsify its meaning, as is indicated by the conversation between Jesus and his disciples which follows it. Note first that to the question, "What good deed must I do . . . ?", Jesus replies: "One there is who is good"—God. That is to say that our "good works" can never satisfy the divine demand; for our best human works are tarnished by egoism, they are never pure. To take the Law seriously—and Jesus takes it very seriously—is to discover our limitations; it is to discover our inability to achieve the goal of the double commandment of love to God and love to our neighbor. In demanding that the rich young man leave all and follow him, Jesus made him aware of the limits of his love; but he opened to him at the same time a way of salvation. Faith in Jesus and his word can alone break a man's bonds and set him free for God. Where his treasure is, there will his heart be (see 6:19-21).

Jesus declares how much the attachment to the treasures of this world possesses men and prevents them from giving themselves completely. How many men have renounced the joys of a life consecrated to the service of God because of anxiety over material security! The saying of verse 24 is hard in its deliberately paradoxical form: "It is easier for a camel to go through the eye of a needle than for a rich man to enter the kingdom of God." The disciples are greatly amazed. They understand that this judgment goes beyond the problem of material riches, for they exclaim: "Who then can be saved?" The reply of Jesus is pointblank: No one, unless God saves him.

We have seen earlier in studying the Sermon on the Mount that Jesus understands the demands of God's Law as driving us into the corner of the impossible. It is a matter of being "born anew," of a conversion of heart which God alone can effect in us. And it is precisely to bring this about that Jesus has come. The new "righteousness" which he reveals and confers goes beyond that of the scribes and Pharisees (5:20). The Kingdom which he announces is open to the "little ones," to the "poor," to those who know that they are nothing and have nothing of themselves and expect everything from God and his grace.

The question of Peter is somewhat naïve. He thinks that he has "left everything" (vs. 27). His denial some weeks later will show that he also is not free from human attachments. He has not measured the cross which awaits him. But Jesus knows Peter's sincerity. He knows that the vocation directed by him to Peter will triumph over all obstacles. And he makes to his Apostles a solemn promise: in the world to come, when the Son of Man "shall sit on his glorious throne," the Apostles who shall have followed him in his earthly pilgrimage and been associated with his sufferings will participate in his reign (see II Tim. 2:11-12). It is they to whom it will be given to judge "the twelve tribes of Israel" (vs. 28; see Luke 22:28-30). Those who for love of Jesus—"for my name's sake"—shall have left their houses, their families, or their lands will receive here below a "a hundredfold" for that which they have lost. For they will be acquainted with this new family which is the community of believers, in which each participates for the good of all and all for the good of each—a fraternal communion of which the Acts and the Letters of Paul give us some examples and which remains characteristic of a church truly alive. It is still only a "sign," certainly, but already a marvelous sign of that perfect communion in the Kingdom which the disciples will one day know.

Verse 30 sounds like a warning given to disciples who are too assured of their future destiny. Those who believe themselves to be first could well be last in the Kingdom, and vice versa. This saying introduces the parable which follows and will be taken up again at its end (20:16).

The Workers Hired at Different Hours (20:1-16)

This parable is often misunderstood. Is not the attitude of the householder manifestly unjust, and is not the indignation of those who have worked from the first hour legitimate? We have seen that Jesus often used paradox to make his hearers react more vigorously. The point of the parable is found in verse 15: "Is your eye evil because I am good?" (see margin). The story can be understood only if the householder is God himself before whom there is no "just wage," for everything that we receive we receive from his mercy. The point of the parable is directed as much against the Pharisee, sure of himself, as against the disciples who boast themselves of being workers from the first hour. The sinner who repents at "the eleventh hour" can enter with them—who knows, before them!—into the glory of the Lord (see 21:31). No one but God knows who will be "first" or "last" in his Kingdom. And those who believe that they enter it "by right" strongly risk being among the last.

Third Announcement of the Passion; The Vocation
of the Servant (20:17-28; Mark 10:32-45)

Jesus and the Twelve approach Jerusalem. Jesus announces for
the third time his approaching Passion, and with more precision
than on preceding occasions.

These repeated prophecies, even if certain details have been
fixed in the tradition after the event, pose a question for us.
How can the complete confusion of the disciples at the time of
the Crucifixion be explained if they had been warned of the course
of events? Why did they not expect the Resurrection? When a
truth completely escapes us, it is not engraved in the memory or
it comes back to us only after a blow. All the Gospels witness
the fact that the disciples continue to have only "human
thoughts." They understand neither the meaning of the words of
Jesus (see Luke 9:45; Mark 9:32; 10:32) nor the sign which the
Transfiguration should have been for them. They are like "blind
men."

Was it necessary that the ways of God should be so totally
hidden from them in order that Jesus might know this deep lone-
liness into which he was to enter more and more up to the final
agony? Man is always alone before true sorrow as before death.
This is a threshold which the deepest human sympathies cannot
cross. The one who has chosen to carry "our sorrows" (Isa. 53:4)
walks absolutely alone, humanly speaking, toward the destiny
which awaits him.

The request of the mother of the sons of Zebedee underscores
still more the disciples' lack of understanding. According to Mark,
it is the disciples themselves who come to present their request
(Mark 10:35). According to Matthew, it is their mother, which
fact somewhat mitigates their responsibility. But they are there,
sure of themselves. James and John are involved, two of the
nearest and most beloved disciples. Their Master is going to death;
but they are speculating on the place to be reserved for them in
the Kingdom—and they ask nothing less than the first place.

The reply of Jesus confronts them with hard reality. Are they
ready to drink with him the cup of death—ready for martyrdom?
They answer, Yes. And Jesus does not dispute their fidelity. (Acts
12:2 testifies to the martyrdom of James.) But the Father alone
assigns to each one the place in the Kingdom which he has prepared for him.

The other ten Apostles are indignant, as though this problem of their place in the Kingdom did not occupy them all (see Mark 9:33-34). Then Jesus calls them together and repeats to them, under a new form, what he has not ceased to tell them since the beginning: he is great who knows himself to be small and humbles himself, who desires to be the servant of all. Jesus sets over against the way of the world—where those who hold authority and power have no other ambition than to dominate—his own way, the way of the Son of Man who makes himself the Servant and willingly dies the death of a slave "as a ransom for many." A ransom is that which a slave or his near relatives paid for his liberation. Jesus here reveals for the first time the redemptive significance of his death—it will free from the power of Satan all those who believe in him.

Jesus knows that the spirit of domination is not peculiar to temporal authority alone, and that the will to power will also be the temptation of the Church (see Luke 22:24-27). He tells us clearly that his way is different, and that he knows no other power than that of the Cross, no other grandeur save that of service.

Healing of Two Blind Men
(20:29-34; Mark 10:46-52; Luke 18:35-43)

Perhaps the joining of this healing with the story which precedes it is not mere happenstance. After having seen the spiritual blindness of the disciples, we are confronted by two poor beggars who cry to Jesus and call him "Son of David"—a Messianic title. The crowd tries in vain to silence them, and Jesus "in pity" grants their request. It is easier for Jesus to give sight to the blind who believe in him than to make the scales fall from the eyes of his disciples who do not know to what degree they are still blind.

The Triumphal Entry (21:1-22)

The Entry Into Jerusalem
(21:1-11; Mark 11:1-10; Luke 19:29-44; John 12:12-19)

All the Gospels see a Messianic act in Jesus' triumphal entry into Jerusalem, the fulfillment of the prophecy of Zechariah (Zech. 9:9). This is why they attach a certain importance to the colt. It is with deliberate purpose that Jesus borrows this mount, and everything about the entry is directed and prepared by God.

But the Gospel by John notes that the disciples understood the meaning of all this only much later (John 12:16). For to mount an ass was in itself nothing either very royal or very glorious. On the contrary it was a sign of humility. The distinctive character of the King announced by Zechariah is that of being "humble" and of bringing "peace" (Zech. 9:9-10). Nevertheless, by this act Jesus affirms his royalty.

Matthew amplifies the story of Mark a little. Influenced no doubt by the text of Zechariah ("riding on an ass, on a colt the foal of an ass"), he mentions both a colt *and* a she-ass. He describes the people coming in crowds to meet Jesus, although Mark only mentions the group of disciples who come with Jesus from Galilee. A too noisy manifestation would certainly have provoked an intervention by the Roman authorities, who feared these popular movements as preludes to insurrection. The Gospels record that the host of the faithful sing their faith and their joy. They recognize in Jesus the Son of David. They likely sang Psalm 118, which belongs to the cycle of Psalms of the great feasts (the Hallel), for one verse of this Psalm is cited: "Blessed be he who comes in the name of the Lord!" (21:9; see Ps. 118:26). The term "Hosanna" signifies "Save now" or "Come to our help!" It may, however, be understood as a form of benediction. The earth and the heavens sing the glory of the One who comes.

To the inhabitants of Jerusalem who are astonished by this triumphant arrival, and ask, "Who is this?" the disciples reply: "This is the prophet Jesus from Nazareth of Galilee." The Messianic secret is not disclosed. The disciples are associated in an act whose significance they do not yet fully grasp.

In the ancient tradition of the Church, Matthew 21:1-11 is read the first Sunday in Advent. It prefigures the glorious coming of the Lord at the last day, when he will enter upon his reign. It echoes Psalm 24:7-10, which celebrated the entrance of the Holy Ark into the city of Jerusalem. This same passage from Matthew is also read on Palm Sunday. It reminds us on each occasion that the King of glory is come into the city to be crucified. His disciples acclaim him, but he knows to what he is going. The Gospel by Luke shows him casting a long look on this city which, in rejecting him, is going to judge itself and to sign its own doom (Luke 19:41-44).

The Merchants Driven from the Temple
(21:12-17; Mark 11:15-18; Luke 19:45-48; John 2:13-17)

The violence of this scene often shocks gentle spirits. According to John, Jesus took a whip! How can this be reconciled with what is told us elsewhere of his gentleness, and with his own words concerning the love of enemies? Let us be thankful that the Gospels have preserved this story for us. Gentleness does not exclude firmness, and love sometimes demands the most unyielding severity. Jesus is not defending himself, he is defending the honor of God. He shudders at seeing God's name and Temple profaned. May God give us to know the righteous wrath which that day animated the Savior, each time the worship of the living God turns into hypocrisy and falsehood! The Temple had become the place of commercial business. Here were the poor, those who could only offer a sacrifice of pigeons, exploited by the merchants and the money-changers. Thus the Law of Leviticus (Lev. 1:14; 5:5-7; 12:8; compare Luke 2:24; with Lev. 14:22 compare Matt. 8:4) became an occasion of plundering the neighbor. Beyond the merchants, the judgment of Jesus strikes at the priests who tolerate these things. For this they will not spare him (see Mark 11:18).

The scene which follows, and which has been preserved only by Matthew, assumes a wholly different character. Some cripples and beggars approach Jesus and he heals them. And then some children take up once more in chorus the cry of the crowds (see 21:9): "Hosanna to the Son of David!" (vs. 15). This Messianic title provokes the indignation of the priests. Jesus replies to them by citing Psalm 8. This is to say clearly that in the Person of Jesus, God himself is present and active. The truth goes out from the mouths of children.

Jesus withdraws to Bethany. According to the Fourth Gospel, that is where Martha and Mary and their brother Lazarus dwelt (John 11:1-2; 12:1-2). It is in this beloved home that Jesus will pass his last nights (see Mark 11:11).

The Barren Fig Tree (21:18-22; Mark 11:12-14, 19-25)

This story is difficult to understand if one does not grasp its symbolic meaning. The tree which had a healthy look was in reality sterile and condemned. Perhaps it is necessary to relate these accounts in Matthew and Mark to the parable in Luke

13:6-9. It is clear that in that parable the fig tree refers to the house of Israel, as is true also in the parable of the Tenants of the Vineyard in Matthew 21:33-41. The cursing of the fig tree is *an enacted parable*. The tree which does not bear fruit will be uprooted. The long patience of God reaches its limit.

The miracle is the occasion of a conversation on prayer. Jesus stresses anew the fact that he who asks in faith, without doubting, receives what he asks for (see 14:31; 17:20). True faith lays hold on the object of prayer as having already received it. Nothing is impossible to the Creator of the heavens and the earth. He is the one who has made the mountains and the sea, who gives life to the trees or takes it away from them. The "mountain" (see the same image in Matt. 17:20) is a figure of things which are impossible for men but possible for God. We sometimes say of our cares that they weigh like "a mountain" on our shoulders. For faith there is no burden so heavy that God cannot lift it. It is of this very concrete and realistic faith that this passage speaks.

Controversies with the Chief Priests, Scribes, and Pharisees (21:23—22:46)

The leaders of Israel are offended by the popularity of Jesus, but because of this very popularity they do not immediately attack him openly. They try rather to make him say some words which will serve as a pretext for a condemnation. Hence, they set snares for him. But the wisdom of God confounds that of men, and Jesus reveals himself as more skillful than they. Sensing their game, he avails himself of their own weapons and with one blow unmasks them.

Of the Authority of Jesus and That of John
(21:23-32; Mark 11:27-33; Luke 20:1-8)

Jesus knows the anger which he is on the verge of stirring up, but he comes nonetheless to teach openly in the Temple. Hence the question: "By what authority are you doing these things . . . ?"

True authority is not proved by arguments; it is recognized, it authenticates itself. For those who have eyes to see or ears to hear, the authority of Jesus manifests itself in his words and his works. We have seen this all through his ministry.

Therefore, Jesus replies to the question by another question: What was the authority of John the Baptist? Indeed, if these men had taken John's baptism of repentance seriously, if they had believed his message, they would have known who Jesus is. The chief priests side-step the question, thus revealing their bad faith.

The parable of the Two Sons with its conclusion (vss. 28-32) is closely connected with that which precedes it. It is preserved only by Matthew. Jesus places their own condemnation in the mouths of his accusers (vss. 30-31); for they are like the son who said, "Yes," but did not obey. John the Baptist had preached the righteousness of God. The tax collectors and harlots had believed his message and repented. They will go into the Kingdom of God before the leaders of Israel. Once again the accent is placed on doing the will of God. What we profess to believe has no value if it is not translated into obedience. This warning is addressed to "religious" people in every age.

The Parable of the Tenants
(21:33-46; Mark 12:1-12; Luke 20:9-19)

This parable calls up the whole drama of Israel, that elect and rebellious people now placed before a final decision. Its meaning is clear for every Jew well versed in the Scriptures, for the image of the vine is used in the Old Testament to designate Israel, and everyone knew from memory the "song of the vineyard" of Isaiah 5:1-7.

But the parable as told by Jesus contained a new point—the sending of the son, introduced by this moving word: "They will respect my son." Without doubt, a human owner would hesitate to risk the life of his son by sending him alone to face some rebels who have just killed his servants! Matthew accentuates the paradox of the situation by saying that finally a group of servants went (vs. 36; compare Luke 20:10-12 where the three servants go one by one; also Mark 12:2-6). This improbable aspect of the story is certainly deliberately designed; for what is more unlikely to the human reason than the sacrifice of the Son of God?

This parable strongly underlines the responsibility of the leaders of Israel. A final appeal has been addressed to them, and they are about to reject it. According to Matthew, which runs counter to Mark and Luke at this point, Jesus poses the judgment of the owner on his tenants under the form of a question (vss. 40-41). Thus the hearers themselves pronounce the verdict —the master of the vineyard will put to death the guilty vinedressers and lease out his vineyard to others.

Jesus states his thought more precisely by means of another image taken from Scripture: that of the stone rejected by the builders which becomes the cornerstone (could the reference be perhaps to the "keystone"?) of the new work built by the Lord himself (vs. 42; see Ps. 118:22-23). Verse 44 (which is not found in certain manuscripts) is connected directly to verse 42; the stone will break those who run against it, but it will crush those on whom it falls (see Isa. 8:14-15). Doubtless in this image of the stone there should be seen an allusion to the old Temple which God is going to destroy and the new Temple which is not made by the hand of man. The Apostles take up this image again on several occasions (Acts 4:11; Rom. 9:33; I Peter 2:4-8).

Verse 43 states precisely that the Kingdom will be taken away from the unfaithful tenants and given to "a nation producing the fruits of it." In reality, this does not refer to a "nation" in the geographical and ethnic sense, but to that "holy nation," the new people, the "race" born from above of which the Apostle Peter speaks (I Peter 2:9-10).

The chief priests understood very well the meaning of these two parables. But, the record tells us, they did not dare to arrest Jesus yet because of the people who sided with him. It was necessary to intrigue behind the scenes and to prepare or bribe public opinion.

When we read these severe judgments of Jesus on the Old Israel, we must not forget that such judgments are directed likewise against the New Israel to the degree to which it ceases to "bear fruit" and betrays its mission. That is what Paul develops with great force in his parable of the Olive Tree (Rom. 11:17-24): "So do not become proud, but stand in awe." What has happened to one part of Israel could happen to you in your turn; useless branches will be cut off (see also John 15:1-7).

The Marriage Feast (22:1-14; Luke 14:16-24)

The two versions of this story in Matthew and in Luke reveal a common basis—the invitation to the feast, the refusal of those invited, the invitation issued then to all who came until the room was full. But the differences are striking and show that we are confronted by two differing traditions taking their rise from the same story. Luke includes some traits which are very lifelike— those invited are too busy; the master of the house invites "the poor and maimed and blind and lame"; then, in a second

sending he enlarges yet further the circle of those invited and declares that none of those who were originally invited shall taste
of the banquet. We find here a well-known theme, a faithful image
of what has happened during Jesus' ministry—the allusion to the
Messianic banquet is evident to those who are initiated, but remains veiled from the others.

The story of Matthew strongly accentuates the Messianic character of the parable. The one who issues the invitation is a king,
and the occasion is a marriage feast. Those who are invited are
not content to decline the invitation; they assassinate the messengers (vs. 6). The king decides to burn the city (vs. 7). It is difficult not to see in this feature an allusion to the burning of Jerusalem in A.D. 70—an interpretation of the parable in the light
of events. The king sends his servants to invite all whom he meets
—"both bad and good." The new community which Jesus comes
to found does not include only the pure!

To this first parable is linked that of the man without the
wedding garment who is cast out (vss. 11-14). What is its meaning? Some interpreters call upon an oriental custom according to
which a garment required for the occasion was delivered to the
invited guests (Gen. 45:22; Judges 14:12-13). Hence, no one was
excusable for not having been clothed with it. But the garment
here likely has a symbolic meaning. God "clothes" us with his
righteousness and his salvation (see Isa. 61:10; Ps. 132:9, 16;
Zech. 3:3-5; Rev. 3:4-5, 18; 19:7-8). The wedding garment shows
that one is a participant in the feast. All ugliness, all sadness,
all impurity, is a discordant intrusion in the wedding chamber.
Thus the children of the Kingdom are known by the joy which
radiates from them. If they do not participate in the feast, they
will be only intruders.

Jesus opens wide the doors of the Kingdom. He calls, he urges
the crowd to enter. But how few respond to the invitation! "For
many are called, but few are chosen."

God and Caesar (22:15-22; Mark 12:13-17; Luke 20:20-26)

This passage is important because men have frequently attempted to build out of this word of Jesus a theory concerning
the State. Let us note first of all that the intention of the Pharisees
is to lay a trap for Jesus, to "entangle" him. The leaders of
the Pharisees refrain from coming in person. They send some
"Herodians," that is to say, some men of the circle of Herod,

who were partisans of his pro-Roman politics. Herod's politics were not at all those of the Pharisees, but every means is good in compelling Jesus to imperil himself by taking sides either for or against Rome. In the popular expectation the coming of the Messiah meant the end of the Roman yoke. If Jesus declares himself for Roman authority, he loses the confidence of the people; if he declares himself against Caesar, he becomes a political insurgent. It is the Messianic problem which is posed here. It was an effort to shut Jesus up to a dilemma. It is then quite justifiable to charge as "hypocrites" those who approach him with flattering words but whose only purpose is to destroy him.

Pious Jews shunned even looking on the image of Caesar. Jesus has no such vain scruples. He takes a coin and shows it to his questioners. He confronts them with their real situation—they are under the dominion of Caesar. Let them, therefore, render to him what is his! But let them also render to God what is God's! We know from elsewhere what Jesus thinks of temporal authority—it is its nature to "domineer" (see 20:25). This domineering is a part of the order of this world which is destined to disappear. The norms of the Kingdom to come are exactly the opposite (20:26-27; see 5:5). But this Kingdom cannot be established by violence; it can be established only by God himself, in his own time. All revolutionary messianism is thus discarded. The authority of Caesar is acknowledged within its proper limits. The Gospel according to John states clearly the thought of Jesus on this point: his Kingdom is not of this world. But God governs history, and temporal authority exists only because he has willed it thus (see John 18:36; 19:10-11). Sovereign and final authority remains that of God. The State can require only our money and our services, never our souls—that is to say, the obedience which we owe only to God.

Of the Resurrection (22:23-33; Mark 12:18-27; Luke 20:27-40)

This time the attack does not come from the Pharisees but from the Sadducees, the representatives of the priestly caste. The resurrection was a subject of controversy among the Jews. Belief in the resurrection appears rarely in the Old Testament and then only in the latest parts, such as the Book of Daniel (Dan. 12:2). The Pharisees believed in it while the Sadducees rejected it, accepting only the authority of the Pentateuch—the original Mosaic Law. On this point Jesus shares the conviction of the

Pharisees. The Sadducees try to prove their argument by an absurd example: To whom will a wife belong who has had seven husbands? The Sadducees are not the only ones who have asked such trifling questions about the beyond. We would all like to pierce the mystery of it. Jesus refuses to reply to this question in the form in which it is posed. He accuses his adversaries of not understanding the Scriptures because they do not believe *in the power of God*. It is a matter of a new creation, of an order of things other than the one here below. Marriage and procreation belong to the order of this world. The angels, by their nature, are not involved in these temporal conditions. Jesus says no more than that. We must receive in faith the affirmation of the life to come, without trying to know more than Jesus has judged it well to tell us.

In the saying which follows (vss. 31-32), Jesus bases his faith in the resurrection on the fact that God is the living God who communicates his life to those who believe on him. Speaking to the Sadducees, who wish to acknowledge only the authority of Moses, Jesus reminds them of the word spoken by God from the midst of the burning bush (Exod. 3:6). Abraham, Isaac, and Jacob are among the living—because they have believed in God (see Matt. 8:11).

Let us note that this conception is totally different from the Greek conception—shared by so many moderns!—according to which the physical body is destroyed and the soul is immortal by nature. For Jesus, eternal life is a gift of God; it is a resurrection from the dead, a wholly new mode of existence, a fullness of being whose form remains veiled from us.

The Great Commandment
(22:34-40; Mark 12:28-34; Luke 10:25-28)

The question of the Pharisees is presented by Matthew as a new attempt to embarrass Jesus (compare the slightly different setting in Mark where the questioner seems sincere). The commandment in Deuteronomy 6:4-5 is recited every day by faithful Jews. Tradition brought together the two commandments of love of God and love of neighbor (Lev. 19:18). Jesus makes no innovation in calling to mind these two commandments, and his adversaries find no basis to counter him, for it is true that the whole Law springs from them. The difference between Jesus and his opponents lies in the fact that "they preach, but do not practice" (23:3). They

do not see that the absoluteness of the divine demand condemns
them. It is this absolute that Jesus has already stressed in the
Sermon on the Mount (see ch. 5). Far from abolishing the ancient
commandment, Jesus makes it the very center of his teaching.
Yet with the same stroke he drives us into the corner of the
impossible.

Who of us loves God with all his heart, with all his soul, with
all his mind, that is, with his whole being? Who of us does not
secretly love himself more than he loves his neighbor? Thus the
Law when reduced to these two commandments is more than ever
our condemnation. It shuts us up to the mercy of God (5:7), to a
life entirely renewed which only his Spirit can create in us. It is
the Pharisees' refusal to confess their bankruptcy and impotence
which shuts them up to an awkward silence.

Son or Lord? (22:41-46; Mark 12:35-37; Luke 20:41-44)

The argument here may seem subtle to us who are not trained
in rabbinic discussions. But it poses an essential question—that
of the humanity and the divinity of the Messiah. Some saw in the
Messiah a temporal king, a descendant of David, who would re-
establish the kingdom of Israel in its ancient glory (see Isa. 9:5-7;
11:1; Jer. 23:5-6; Ezek. 34:23-24); others, laying stress upon Daniel 7:13-14 and on the Book of Enoch, were looking for a pre-
existent "son of man" who would come from heaven as Judge and
King.

Several times Jesus had been called "Son of David" and did
not reject the title (see 20:31; 21:9, 15; compare 1:1). His descent
from David never seems to have been contested (see Rom. 1:3).
But in calling himself the "Son of man," in announcing his return
as King and Judge of men, he affirms his divine authority (16:27-
28; 25:31-32). In this double human and divine nature lies the
mystery of his Person. He poses the enigma to the Pharisees by
citing Psalm 110, which was acknowledged by tradition as a
Messianic Psalm. How can the Son of David be at the same time
David's Lord? The question is left without reply. Jesus will
openly proclaim his Messiahship only later at his trial (26:63-64).

The Pharisees Judged by Jesus (23:1-39)

The Gospel by Matthew is unique in retaining in its entirety
this severe discourse, the most severe which Jesus ever pro-

nounced. In considering it, let us remember that Jesus addressed these reproaches to the most "churchgoing" believers of his day. All false piety, all piety which does not translate itself into action, was abhorrent to Jesus because it is an insult to the living God. The danger of such aberrations is present in every age, and the history of Christianity is not exempt from them. Is any one of us wholly exempt? To be "true" implies a total harmony of thought, word, and act, a total freedom from pretense. It is this harmony and this transparency which give to Jesus his unique authority. Everything is "Yes" in him as it is in God (II Cor. 1:19). That is why in his presence we can only acknowledge ourselves sinners and wait for him to re-create us in his image. The sin of the Pharisees is in their refusal to acknowledge Jesus for what he is; that would oblige them to acknowledge themselves for what they are. We must listen to his warnings as addressed to ourselves.

"They Preach, But Do Not Practice" (23:1-12)

The scribes and Pharisees "sit on Moses' seat." They are charged to teach, which is always a solemn responsibility (compare James 3:1). Jesus does not here dispute their teaching, but says: "Practice and observe whatever they tell you." Once again this verifies his respect for the Scriptures. What he objects to in the Pharisees, however, is that "they preach, but do not practice." Their legalism weighs on the faithful like an intolerable burden, but they themselves find ways to circumvent the Law. They love to play a part; they love to "be seen by men" (6:1-6). They parade their piety by magnifying its external marks —"phylacteries" were bands, fastened on the forehead and arm, on which some verses of the Law were inscribed (see Deut. 6:4-9); "fringes" on their garments were a sign of the consecration of Israel to her God (Num. 15:37-40).

Jesus himself seems to have complied with this last custom, as did all Jews, for we are told on two occasions that someone touched "the fringe" of his garment (9:20; 14:36). It is, then, not the custom itself that he condemned, but the ostentation of those who do these things merely to be seen. The Pharisees seek everywhere to occupy the "place of honor"; they crave the honors which they consider to belong to their rank. They have themselves called "rabbi," from a word signifying "great." Celebrated rabbis received the title "Abba," or Father.

In verses 8-12 he addresses himself directly to his disciples. No one among them is to be called "great," for One only is great, One only is their Master, One only is their Father and they are all "brothers." Likewise, One only is their Master or Leader—the Christ. The characteristic mark of the new community lies in the fact that he who is greatest makes himself the servant of his brothers: "Whoever exalts himself will be humbled, and whoever humbles himself will be exalted." Here again is found a fundamental thought which has already been expressed on several occasions (20:25-28; 19:30; 20:16; Luke 14:7-11).

Do these words of Jesus exclude all gradations of office in the Church? Certainly not. Jesus himself established the primacy of the Apostles in the nascent community (16:18; 19:28; 28:16-20). But in the sight of God he only is great who knows himself to be small, a sinner redeemed, as are all his brothers, solely by the grace of God. All human authority is only delegated. One alone is Lord, One alone is Father—God; One alone has authority to govern us in God's name—Jesus Christ.

Jesus knows that the demons of pride and power which blind the religious leaders of his people will also menace, ever anew, his Church. He does not tire of putting his disciples on guard against this deadly snare and reminding them continually of the humility of the Servant.

"Woe to You . . . !"(23:13-39)

This "Woe to you . . . !" is repeated seven times—eight times if verse 14, which is found in certain manuscripts, is included. These woes are like a negative counterpart of the Beatitudes: Jesus opens the Kingdom, the Pharisees shut it.

Jesus describes the scribes and Pharisees as "hypocrites." This term in the original language signifies an inconsistent attitude of which the one who adopts it is not necessarily conscious but which renders his behavior false, objectively speaking. In what sense did the Pharisees close the Kingdom of heaven to their followers? Jesus does not upbraid them for taking the Law seriously. He takes it more seriously than they (see Matt. 5:17-20). But if they had truly understood the Scriptures, they would have recognized in Jesus the One who comes to liberate men from the condemnation of the Law. They crushed others under a yoke which they themselves could not bear (see vs. 4). Not only did they refuse the good news of salvation, they also deterred others from believing it. Verse 14 underlines the contradiction between the Pharisees' lack of charity and their "long prayers" (on the "widows," see Exod. 22:22-23; Isa. 1:17). Verse 15 accuses them of having a false missionary zeal, for in weighing down the Gentiles under their Law they make them children of "Gehenna" (see margin; the term "Gehenna" comes from the Valley of Hinnom where refuse was thrown). The thought of Jesus here seems to be very near that of Paul, who sees the knowledge of the Law as an intensification of condemnation (see Rom. 2:12-16; 7:7-13).

Verses 16-22 take up again the question of oaths which was raised earlier (5:33-37). By subtle distinctions the Pharisees have succeeded in making perjury legitimate. One is not bound unless he swears by the *gold* of the Temple or by the *offering* which is on the altar. Jesus overthrows all considerations established in this fashion: the Temple and the altar are consecrated to God; they are signs of his presence. Who swears by them calls on God as a witness. This is exactly the same as swearing by heaven, which is the throne of God. The casuistry of the Pharisees proves their blindness. The real meaning of worship offered to God escapes them.

Verses 23-24 point out another flagrant inconsistency. The Pharisees are very careful to pay the tithe even on the little herbs, but they neglect the weighty matters of the Law. They filter their wine so as not to swallow an impure gnat, but they swallow "a camel"! For they trample under foot the two great commandments—love to God and neighbor.

The Law requires that they should cleanse not only the outside of cups and plates but the interior as well. Jesus uses this image (vss. 25-26) to stress once more that the hearts of the Pharisees remain impure and that the real issue is that they be cleansed (see Matt. 15:7-20).

Sepulchres were whitewashed in order that no one defile himself in walking over them; they were polished anew for the influx of pilgrims, in order that they should be "beautiful." Jesus compares the Pharisees to these whitewashed sepulchres which contain only corpses (vss. 27-28). This saying seems singularly hard. In considering it one must understand that for Jesus he who does not live the life given by God, he whose life is shut against love, is *a dead person* with only the appearance of life (compare Eph. 2:1-10).

The scribes and Pharisees gladly honored the tombs of the
prophets by erecting monuments to them (vs. 29). This was a
way of clearing themselves of the crimes committed by their
ancestors! But this attempt at justification gives evidence that
they have the blood of murderers in their veins; for it was precisely against such self-justification that the prophets never ceased
to raise their voice.

Verse 32 is particularly serious. Jesus makes it clear that the
Pharisees are not going to be long in crowning the work of their
fathers. They will kill him as their fathers have killed the prophets. The serpent is traditionally a figure of the Devil; it crawls in
the dust and attacks cunningly.

Jesus has charged us not to judge (see Matt. 5:22; 7:1). Nevertheless, he accuses the Pharisees of being blind people, fools
(23:17), a race of vipers (23:33). Once again this passage sets
forth the consciousness which Jesus has of his sovereign authority. He is the King and the Judge of men. He at the same time
reads their hearts and lays them bare. God speaks by his mouth
and gives to his words the terrible accent of a last warning.

Verses 34-35 present some difficulties. Who is the "I"? It can
hardly be Jesus; it is rather God himself. The parallel passage in
Luke (11:49) puts this saying into the mouth of "the Wisdom of
God." Does this refer to one of the Wisdom books which is now
lost? Or does it refer to God himself, reciting a summary of the
crimes committed by Israel? The end of verse 34 which speaks of
some who will be scourged in the synagogues seems to echo the
persecutions undergone by the Primitive Church. Finally, the
description of the murder of "Zechariah" calls to mind II Chronicles 24:17-21, although the description "son of Barachiah" seems
to refer to the prophet Zechariah (see Zech. 1:1-2).

The important thing, however, is not the answer to these prob-
lems. The history of the People of God has a tragic aspect which
the Bible strongly underlines. The natural man is in rebellion
against God; he is a murderer from the beginning (see Gen. 4:1-
10). The Israel according to the flesh stands against the Israel
according to faith in every age. It was because Abel was "righteous" in the eyes of God that Cain could not endure his presence
(see Gen. 4:1-10; I John 3:12). It was because Zechariah was
"righteous" and spoke in the power of the Spirit that he was
stoned (see II Chron. 24:20-21). Hence, the murder of the only
Son will be the logical conclusion, the culminating point, of all

the murders of history. The revolt of man against God will reach its zenith in "this generation" (vs. 36). Jesus is the Innocent One, the Righteous One par excellence, of whom all the others were only annunciatory signs; their murder, so to speak, is included in his own.

The judgment which Jesus has just pronounced wrings from him a cry whose poignant accent strongly contrasts with what has gone before (vss. 37-39). All his love for the Holy City, the object of all his appeals and promises, bursts forth in the lament: "O Jerusalem, Jerusalem, killing the prophets . . . How often would I have gathered your children together . . ." This expression implies repeated appeals of which the first three Gospels give only a few echoes. Historic truth at this point seems to be more accurately reflected in the Gospel according to John, which shows Jesus going up to Jerusalem on several occasions, notably at the time of the great feasts, to exercise his ministry there (see John 2:13; 5:1; 7:14; 10:22-23; 12:12). This alone can explain the saying, "How often would I . . . and you would not!" The image of gathering under the "wings" is used several times in the Old Testament to express the maternal solicitude of God (see Deut. 32:10-11; Pss. 36:7; 91:4).

Salvation has been proclaimed to Jerusalem, and Jerusalem has refused the grace offered. It must therefore experience, at least for a time, what Zechariah prophesied: "Because you have forsaken the LORD, he has forsaken you" (II Chron. 24:20). The "house" which is "forsaken and desolate" may designate the Temple or the city, or it may refer symbolically to the entire country.

This discourse nevertheless concludes on a positive note (vs. 39): Jerusalem will see her rejected King again when he comes in his glory. All will acclaim him on that day as the One sent by the Lord. The words are the same as those used at the Triumphal Entry (21:9).

THE ACCOMPLISHMENT

Matthew 24:1—28:20

The final conversations of Jesus with his disciples deal with the end of the world and his return in glory. Thus the Lord warns and fortifies his own before his Passion and turns their gaze to-

ward the New Age when, having participated in his struggles
and sufferings, they will participate in his glory.

Discourse on the End of the Age (24:1-41)

The Destruction of the Temple (24:1-2)

The Temple, begun by Herod the Great forty-six years earlier
(see John 2:20), was of impressive dimensions, and the disciples
do not hide their admiration of it. The words of Jesus must have
struck them with a shock. The days of this glorious edifice are
numbered and all its glory is only vanity!

These words of Jesus echo those of the prophets (Micah 3:9-
12; Jer. 7:4, 12-15; 26:4-6, 17-19). The first Temple had been,
in fact, destroyed in 587 B.C., but that judgment was remote and
forgotten. The judgment declared by Jesus is considered as a
blasphemy by the Jews of his day. His words spoken to the disciples must have been reported to the Jewish leaders, for they are
cited, albeit in a twisted way, at his trial (26:61; see also John
2:18-22).

Jesus' thought here without doubt goes beyond the mere fact
of a material destruction—the age of the old Temple, of the old
worship, is at an end; a new era has begun. Indeed, the place of
divine revelation is now the Person of Jesus: "something greater
than the temple is here" (Matt. 12:6). This is the interpretation
which is explicitly given by the Fourth Gospel, but it makes clear
that the meaning of these words will be understood only after
the Resurrection. Matthew reports only the imminent judgment.
The Temple was in fact destroyed at the time of the burning of
Jerusalem in A.D. 70.

The Disciples Question Jesus on the End of the World (24:3-14)

Jesus is seated with his disciples on the Mount of Olives, opposite the city. The judgment which he has just pronounced
troubles the disciples. By their question, "Tell us, when will
this be . . .?" they seem to comprise in one three distinct events—
the destruction of the Temple, the precursory signs of the coming
of the Messiah, and the end of the world.

According to Jewish tradition it was on the Mount of Olives
that God would take up his position at the last day to wage war
against the nations and manifest his Kingship (see Zech. 14).

After the apocalypse of Daniel the time of this "coming" was a constant object of speculation. The Greek term for "arrival" or "advent" was used to describe the coming of a monarch such as Caesar, who was treated as a god. The reference here then is to the coming of Jesus as King and Judge.

From the very first Jesus puts his disciples on guard against false messiahs (vss. 4-5; see vss. 23-24). We know from the historian Josephus that during this epoch there was a series of nationalistic leaders who had Messianic pretensions. The upheavals of the years 66-70 were due to hopes of this sort. And at the time of the insurrection in the years 132-135 one named Bar Cochba was identified by some as the Messiah. Jesus did not cease to put his followers on guard against the danger of political messianism. This problem is not peculiar to Jewish messianism. It appears anew in history under various forms each time that men claim to achieve spiritual ends by temporal force and so present themselves as "saviors" of their nation. We are warned that many men will be seduced by such false messiahs.

To this first warning Jesus immediately adds a second—the catastrophes of history are not in themselves evidence that the end of the world is near (vss. 6-7). Wars, famines, tremblings of the earth, were regarded by the prophets as warnings, as punishments from God. This note never ceases to resound throughout the Old Testament, and the Jewish apocalypses re-echo it. Jesus underlines the inevitability of crises. He certainly does not intend either to justify war or to invite us to resign ourselves to evil. He simply states that in a world in revolt against God, a world of hate and violence, such explosions are in the logic of things, and should not trouble our faith. It will not be necessary to conclude too quickly that the end of the world is near. We well know why such warning was necessary. At each war or threat of war we see predictions of all sorts arising to trouble credulous spirits!

Jesus compares the "last times" to pangs of childbirth (vs. 8; see Isa. 26:16-21). These increase in intensity until the child is born. Thus the adverse forces will arise with increasing violence against the children of the Kingdom. We find here again the warnings given at the time when the disciples were sent out (10:16-23) but now intensified. Some will deny their faith and become informers against their brothers. Hence confusion will reign in the midst of the Church itself.

The term which is translated "wickedness" in verse 12 means

literally "absence of law" or "violation of the law." It describes the total anarchy which rages where no norm is any longer respected. At such a time "most men's love will grow cold." The basic law which governs the disciples of Jesus is the love of God and neighbor (see 22:34-40). The victory of the Cross is the victory of God over all the forces of hate and death. But such will be the power of evil that many—"most"!—will be carried away by the current; they will reject the Cross. Everything which kills the love within us—and war always engenders hatred of the enemy—kills the soul. The danger of persecution and injustice is not physical death but this sort of death.

"But he who endures to the end will be saved" (vs. 13). To endure is to hold fast; it is to observe the Word of God and count on his fidelity whatever be the unfurling and the apparent triumph of contrary forces (see Rev. 3:10-11). The possibility of falling remains for the Christian to the very end. This is why he must fear temptation (see Matt. 6:13) and know that at every moment if he were abandoned to his own human strength he could only perish (see 24:22).

Whatever be the power of evil let loose by the Adversary, the purpose of God will nonetheless be fulfilled. The good news of the Kingdom, the announcement of its coming, must be proclaimed to the ends of the earth (vs. 14). All must know the message of salvation. Thus the proclamation of this salvation becomes a preliminary condition to the end of the world. It is in this sense—and in this sense only—that believers can "hasten" the day of the coming of the Lord (see II Peter 3:3-13).

Matthew 24:14, which is given only in this Gospel, is very important because it stresses as no other the eschatological importance of the missionary task entrusted by Jesus to his disciples (see also 28:18-19). We have seen earlier several times that of all the Gospels, Matthew is the most deeply rooted in Jewish tradition; yet he is at the same time strongly missionary. In this he is faithful to the prophetic tradition which sees Israel as the witness of God among the nations (Gen. 12:3; Isa. 2:2-4; 49:6; 52:7-10; 60:1-3). He has first shown Jesus concentrating all his efforts on the Elect People and gathering around him the "remnant" on which he is going to build the New Israel of tomorrow (10:5-8; 11:20-24; 15:24; 23:37-39). He shows him now entrusting to his disciples the evangelization of the Gentiles, opening the gates of the Kingdom to the whole world (see 8:11-12).

In retaining these two phases of the ministry of Jesus, Matthew, more than the other evangelists, puts his finger at the same time on both the grandeur and the tragedy of the unique mission of Israel. "Salvation is from the Jews" (see John 4:22), but this salvation embraces the world. And the rejection of it remains possible to the end of time—as much for those called tomorrow as for those called yesterday.

Days of Distress and Judgment (24:15-41)

This prophecy is inspired directly by the Book of Daniel. It seems to comprise both the ruin of Jerusalem and the end of the world. In reality, the scene is situated in Judea (vs. 16). A shocking sacrilege will be the sign that the hour is come. According to Daniel 9:27 and 11:31, this refers to a profanation of the Temple where the destroyer will celebrate his idolatrous worship on the very altar of God. The Jews kept the burning memory of the sacrilege of Antiochus Epiphanes who, after dreadful massacres, had placed the statue of Jupiter Olympus in the Temple, destroyed the Books of the Law, and forced all the inhabitants of Jerusalem into apostasy on pain of death (168 B.C.).

The passage here announces similar events. We know in fact that in the year A.D. 38 the Emperor Caligula planned to erect his own statue in the Temple in Jerusalem. Death alone prevented him. In the year A.D. 70 the Emperor Titus placed a statue on the site of the burned Temple.

The expectation of an antichrist who would bring iniquity to its zenith marked the first Christian generation (see II Thess. 2:3-12). The same theme is to be found again in the Revelation (Rev. 13).

What should we Christians of the twentieth century retain of these warnings? Let it be said at the very outset that they are not to be bound to a determined chronology. The numbers which are found in Daniel (ch. 12) and in the Revelation (Rev. 13:18) have occasioned vain speculations. Jesus himself has told us that no one but the Father—not even the Son!—knows when the last time will come (24:36). The crises of history remind us that God is not mocked, that the battle between God and Satan continues to the end. There are some moments when evil unfurls itself with such force that Jesus advises his own to flee, not for fear of death but because resistance would be vain. It is up to the Church to determine whether such a moment is come.

The problem is contemporary. We have seen many an instance of men obliged to flee their country in fidelity to their faith, whether it be Huguenots, English Puritans, or more recent examples. Jesus himself escaped from his adversaries several times before his "hour" was come. The Book of the Acts shows all the Christians save the Apostles scattering at the time of a great persecution, and this became for them the occasion for carrying the gospel elsewhere (Acts 8:1-5). At the time of the capture of Jerusalem in A.D. 70 the Christians fled and took refuge in Pella. The passage here is doubtless not unrelated to this event. Jesus tells us not to look for martyrdom but to submit to it if God calls us to it. It is a matter of discernment and obedience.

The discourse of Matthew, like the parallel passages in Mark and Luke, underlines the suddenness of the crisis which will demand a precipitous departure (24:17-21; see Mark 13:15-19; Luke 17:31; 21:23-24). The mention of the Sabbath in verse 20 shows that among Jewish Christians, Sabbath observance had been maintained; hence, they are enjoined to pray that the catastrophe not happen on that day. The allusion to the siege of Jerusalem is clearer in the Gospel by Luke than in the other two (see Luke 21:24).

Verse 22 stresses the fact that the final trial will be such that no one can be sure of resisting it. God, in his mercy, will shorten it so that the elect will not be tempted beyond their strength. His fidelity is the only guarantee of our fidelity in the hour when trial swoops down upon us; but his fidelity is certain (see Rom. 8:31-39). Thus again the warning is accompanied by a promise.

Verse 23 returns to the theme of false messiahs already broached in verse 5. The characteristic mark of false prophets or false messiahs will be that they will imitate the actions of Christ; they will astonish the world by their power of seduction, by their "miracles," thus throwing believers themselves into uncertainty. But if the first coming of the Son of Man was secret, the second will assert itself with the suddenness of lightning. Doubt will not be possible (see Rev. 1:7).

Verse 28 is likely a recollection of a word from the Book of Job (Job 39:27-30). Just as the piercing eye of vultures discerns a dead body from afar, so the judgment will be sudden and inevitable and no one can elude it, no matter where he may be (see Luke 17:37).

The judgment thus described has a cosmic significance. Even

the heavens are shaken, the sun is darkened, the stars fall. This passage draws its inspiration directly from the Old Testament and the Jewish apocalypses. The old world is destroyed to make room for the New Creation (vs. 29; see Mark 13:24-25; Luke 21:25-26; Isa. 13:9-13; 34:4). The Son of Man appears, according to the prophecy of Daniel (7:13-14), to judge the earth and gather the elect.

How is the mourning (vs. 30) which will break forth at his appearing to be interpreted? This is the place to recall the moving prophecy of Zechariah: "And I will pour out on the house of David and the inhabitants of Jerusalem a spirit of compassion and supplication, so that, when they look on him whom they have pierced, they shall mourn for him, as one mourns for an only child, and weep bitterly over him, as one weeps over a first-born" (Zech. 12:10). These are tears not of despair but of repentance, "of compassion and supplication." Jerusalem will know "him whom they have pierced," and "the tribes of the earth" will lament not having recognized him. But may we not believe that a spirit of compassion and supplication will descend on them too at the last hour—the hour of the great gathering of the elect? (see Rev. 1:4-8). The One who has come in the obscurity of the Incarnation under the figure of the crucified Servant will be revealed to all eyes in the brightness of his divine glory. But the glorified Christ has pierced hands (see Luke 24:39; John 20:27; Rev. 5:6). A very ancient tradition pictures the Son of Man appearing in the heavens, stretching his arms above the world in the form of a cross. The trumpet of judgment, the gathering from the "four winds," are classic symbols of the Last Judgment (vs. 31; see Isa. 27:13; I Thess. 4:16; I Cor. 15:52; Rev. 8:2-6; Dan. 7:2; Rev. 7:1-3).

The parable of the Fig Tree in verses 32-33 expresses the same thought as the one on the signs of the times in 16:1-3. Men know how to read the signs of nature. The young leaves on the fig tree announce the heat of summer. Likewise, "these things" of which Jesus has just spoken are an announcement of his coming. By "these things" it is doubtless necessary to understand not so much the final manifestations, since they will be immediate and unforeseeable (see vss. 27, 42), as the struggles, the persecutions, and the seductions which precede them.

The Christian knows that "the last times" have begun at the coming of Jesus Christ into this world. However long should be the duration, we are already in the end-time, marked both by the advent of his reign and by a stiffening of the opposition of the Adversary. The hand-to-hand combat of the sons of the Kingdom with the powers of evil is intensifying, and each episode in this struggle carries in itself the marks of the final assault and triumph. To discern the signs of the times is to penetrate the meaning of current history from the standpoint of this end toward which it moves and which is already near; for brief is our life and brief the life of this world. The Christian is a man who knows himself on the edge of eternity.

Verse 34 poses a question which we have already raised several times. Did Jesus believe in an imminent end of the world? Or should the word "generation" be interpreted with a different meaning than that which it has in our speech? In Greek it can mean "species." If thus translated, then, the word could signify "this people," the Jewish people (on the term "generation" see 12: 41-42; 16:4). First in the order of election, the Jewish people will live to the day when the One whom they have rejected will be manifested in power and glory and they will be constrained to acknowledge him (see Rom. chs. 9-11; Phil. 2:9-11). This second interpretation seems to be quite in accord with this Gospel (see 23:39; 10:23; 26:64).

"Heaven and earth," that is to say, the form of this present world, will pass away. But the words of Jesus will never pass away, for they have living power. Whoever believes them is born into the life eternal (vs. 35; see Mark 13:31; John 6:63, 68).

Verse 36 is very important, for it emphasizes the fact that the Father alone fixes and knows the "day and hour" of the end of the world. The Son himself is subordinate to the Father with regard to this day; the angels are ignorant of it. How much more is it concealed from men! Those who seek to calculate this day pretend to a knowledge which God has judged it well to keep secret. They succumb to a forbidden curiosity. We would all do well to remember this. Is it perhaps objected that the Gospel has just described the "signs" of the end? But this is done in a fashion to make us take seriously this end as *always near*, as *already present* in the struggles of each moment, yet nonetheless hidden.

The example of Noah calls to mind the suddenness of the Judgment. Men ate, drank, married, as they do today, without great concern for the morrow. They thought no more about the Flood than we think seriously about atomic war. For the heedlessness of men is stronger than all the warnings which both nature and history give us in profusion. It is this false security which the prophets continued to denounce throughout the time of the Old Israel. And it is still this false security on the part of the religious people of his time which Jesus seeks to destroy, for he regards it as fatal. No one, he tells us, knows in advance who will be "taken" and who will be "left" of two companions in work laboring in the same field, or of two women at the same millstone. Only Noah was "ready" at the time of the Flood; the others were swept away. The important thing, then, is—"Watch."

"Watch Therefore" (24:42—25:46)

The theme "Watch" is here developed in a series of parables. All pose the same question under different forms: When the Son of Man comes, will he find his own "ready"?

The Parable of the Thief in the Night (24:42-44)

The paradoxical image which compares the coming of the Lord to that of a thief in the night must have struck the first disciples with singular force, for we find it in a succession of passages (see Luke 12:39; I Thess. 5:2; Rev. 3:3; 16:15). Judaism tended to regard the coming of the Messiah as a day terrible for the pagans but glorious for Israel. Christianity has not always escaped a similar illusion. The warning of Jesus, however, is not addressed primarily to pagans but rather to the disciples. The house is entrusted to them: do they know how to take care of it? Will they be wide-awake at the sudden irruption of the Lord who will surprise them as a thief in the night?

Parable of the Faithful or Wicked Servant (24:45-51)

The "faithful and wise" servant is a steward to whom the master has entrusted the management of his household. He is charged with giving out food to the servants and watching over them. Such a role is attributed to Moses in the Old Testament. He is the servant of God of whom the Lord declares: "He is entrusted with all my house" (Num. 12:7; see Heb. 3:5-6). It is possible that in this passage Jesus is thinking particularly of the responsibility of his Apostles; but all Christians are "his household," his possession. Blessed are those whom the Master will find faithful at the post which he has entrusted to them! He will entrust to them all his possessions; they will take part in his reign. But woe to him who takes advantage of the absence of the master to abuse his power and give way to his passions. He will be condemned with "the hypocrites." We have seen that this is the term which Jesus applied to the Pharisees; it describes the flagrant contradiction between what they in reality were and what they pretended to be (23:3, 13, 15, 23, 27, 29-31). It is on the "hypocrites" that the worst condemnation rests (23:33; see 24:51).

Foolish and Wise Maidens (25:1-13)

The picture is that of a wedding. The retinue of maidens provided with torches awaits the coming of the bridegroom to escort the couple into the marriage chamber. Certain old manuscripts mention both "the bridegroom and the bride." But the meaning of the parable is without doubt eschatological; the figure of the bridegroom is often applied to Christ in the New Testament (see Matt. 9:15; John 3:29; II Cor. 11:2; Eph. 5:25; Rev. 19:6-9). It relates to the expectation of his return. He comes in the middle of the night. This feature recalls the preceding parables.

The maidens are not blamed for being asleep. The contrast is between those whom the sudden call finds *ready* and those who are not. In this last hour the former can no longer do anything for the latter. In the hour of judgment each one can respond only for himself. The harshness of the reply of the wise maidens is only the assertion of a fact.

The oil here is a symbol of fidelity and perseverance. To be "wise" in the language of the Bible is to put all one's faith and hope in God—"the righteous and the wise and their deeds are in the hand of God" (Eccl. 9:1). The "fool," the senseless one, is the one who does not believe in God, or who lives as though he does not believe in God (see Ps. 14:1; 53:1-2; Eph. 5:14-16).

Jesus speaks of those whose love "will grow cold" under trial (24:12). The Revelation mentions those who have lost their first love and whose candle will be removed (Rev. 2:4-5). That which was once a brilliant light is so no longer, because of a lack of oil, and its smoking wick is almost extinguished. The first love is dead, and with it dies faith.

The Talents Entrusted to the Servants (25:14-30)

Note first of all that each servant is given responsibilities consistent with his capacities. Two of them double the capital entrusted to them. The third buries his talent and returns it just as it is. The point of the parable is expressed in verse 29: he who does not make productive the gifts he has received *loses* them; they are "taken away" from him. What is to be understood by the "talents"? All our gifts come from God, whether they be natural riches or gifts of the Spirit. We shall have to render account at the last day for our use of these gifts, for the zeal which we shall have put into the service of our Lord. It is of little importance whether we have received much or little.

The reward of the faithful servant is to "enter into the joy" of his master. This is the joy of the Kingdom, of the Messianic banquet. The faithful worker participates in the joy of the Master; this is his supreme reward. He enters with him into the banquet hall. But he who has buried the talent entrusted to him—either through hatred of his Master or through laziness—will not participate in this joy. He is not present at the feast. He is cast out into the darkness of solitude and bitterness reserved for those who have devoted themselves neither to God nor to men. Each one of us is faced with the question: What account shall I render at the last day? Have I buried many favors and many gifts?

The World Judged by the Son of Man (25:31-46)

This picture of the Last Judgment has a particular solemnity. The Son of Man—the One whom men have rejected and crucified—is set forth in all his glory as King and Judge. All nations are summoned before his throne. The angels are subject to him and surround him like a heavenly court.

The image of the shepherd (vs. 32) is inspired by the prophet Ezekiel (ch. 34, particularly vss. 17-24). It is a familiar image which in the Old Testament designates the kings of Israel appointed by God, the Sovereign Shepherd, to care for his people. Jesus here explicitly declares himself King of Israel and King of the world. God has handed over to him the Kingdom and the judgment. He has power to welcome, in the name of the Father, those for whom the Kingdom has been prepared "from the foundation of the world."

Who are the "blessed" of the Father? The criterion employed by Jesus is not at all that which theologians eagerly use, and there is something about it which at first glance is baffling. Jesus does not say what we should have expected: "those who have believed on me," or again, "those who have faithfully served the

Church and frequented the sacraments." No. He says, "I was hungry and you gave me food." The "righteous" to whom he speaks—and they could well be pagans—have no consciousness of ever having done this. And then comes this sovereign word: "As you did it to one of the least of these my brethren, you did it to me."

This has sometimes been interpreted as though the "least" here mentioned were disciples. This narrows the meaning too much. Jesus identifies himself with each poor person, with each suffering one, because on the cross he truly took each one's place. He has taken on himself the burden and the sin of all men. That is why he can say in very truth: what you have done to one of your brothers you have done to me. And inversely: what you have not done to your brothers you have refused to do to *me*.

Does this passage, then, present a religion of works? No, for every act of love has its source in God. It is by such acts that we reveal to whom we belong, whether we are of God or of the Devil. The total teaching of the Sermon on the Mount and the whole of Jesus' severity toward the Pharisees have already indicated that the children of God are recognized by the way in which they practice mercy, and that it is by this fundamental attitude that they will be judged. He who does not love may hold the most orthodox beliefs, but he is still in death (see I John 2:9-11).

This passage is no less upsetting. At the last day Jesus acknowledges as his own, people who have not known him but who have, without knowing it, served him in the person of their suffering neighbor. What a discovery! What a marvelous meeting! But what will he say to us who know him? How many times will we have passed by him without *recognizing* him? He comes to us under the figure of the stranger, the refugee, the man of another race, or the sorry bore. And we turn away, or treat such persons with humiliating conceit. One day he will say to us: "That was I." Could he not then say to us: "You pretend to know me, but I do not know you"? (see 7:23).

The Passion (26:1—27:66)

The Plot Against Jesus and the Deed of a Woman (26:1-16)

Jesus knows that the hour is near—"after two days." It is at the Feast of the Passover that he must die. Having revealed to his disciples all that they need to know, he terminates his teaching (vs. 1). And this teaching will find its fulfillment in his death. He is the new Passover which will be sacrificed for the salvation of the world (see I Cor. 5:7). The evangelist is careful to indicate by this prediction of Jesus that everything is carried out in conformity with the plan of God. The plot which is hatched in the darkness is set down in this plan. Everything happens at the appointed hour. This, however, removes nothing of the guilt of those who plot this death and are its immediate cause.

That this death is a denial of justice is thrown into relief by the secret character of the deliberations of the priests and elders (vss. 3-5). They fear the reactions of the Galilean crowds who come to Jerusalem for the feast. It is necessary that everything be done quickly and without their knowledge.

The story of the anointing at Bethany is inserted into that of the plot against Jesus' life like a ray of light piercing the thick darkness. We have seen that during this last week of his life Jesus withdrew each evening to the little village of Bethany (21:17). The Gospels by Mark and Matthew situate the scene in the house of "Simon the leper" (vs. 6; Mark 14:3), doubtless a man whom Jesus had healed and whose name was known. On the contrary, the name of the woman is passed by in silence by those recorders (see John 12:1-8). The woman pours out her perfume on the head of Jesus. In the thought of the evangelist, this act has a Messianic significance. The royal anointing is given to the One who is about to die. He is indeed "the King of the Jews" but a crucified King. Jesus himself declares that this perfume is poured out in advance to prepare him "for burial," the burial which custom refuses to executed criminals. The woman certainly does not have knowledge of the import of her act. But at the hour when the Master is about to be abandoned by some and betrayed by others, it is given to her—and to her alone—to witness to her faith and love for him. The disciples immediately criticize her. What a waste! But Jesus defends and justifies her: "She has done a beautiful thing." True love does not calculate the outlay. This woman has seized the unique hour which will not happen again. This act will be known "in the whole world," wherever the good news will be preached. From century to century, we will bless the memory of this woman. Does she not incarnate the faithful Church in the hour of supreme abandonment?

"Then one of the twelve, who was called Judas Iscariot" (vs. 14)—thus, without transition, the Gospel leads us from the light of faith into the darkness of treason. Judas "delivers" his Master for "thirty pieces of silver." In other words, he agrees to notify the priests when a favorable occasion presents itself for seizing Jesus when there is no time to alert the crowds.

The Last Supper and the Treachery of Judas (26:17-29)

The institution of the Passover is described in detail in Exodus 12. It was the greatest feast of the year. It commemorated the great deliverance of Israel, her passage from slavery to liberty. It was celebrated by families. They ate the paschal lamb in remembrance of the one whose blood had preserved the Israelites from the wrath of God (Exod. 12:12-14).

According to the Synoptic Gospels, the paschal meal of Jesus with his disciples took place on the first day of the feast, as custom required (26:17; Mark 14:12; Luke 22:7). According to John, it was the evening before the first day (John 13:1; 18:28; 19:14). On this view, Jesus would have been crucified on the same day that the paschal lamb was sacrificed. The information given by John is doubtless the more probable, for it is difficult to imagine the chief priests arresting Jesus once the feast had commenced, that is, after six o'clock in the evening. If John is right, then Jesus advanced the paschal celebration with his disciples one day. It is perhaps necessary to see a sign pointing in this direction in the explanation which Jesus gives to the master of the house who is going to lend him his quarters: "My time is at hand; I will keep the passover at your house with my disciples" (vs. 18). Jesus knows that his hours are numbered. The decisive hour, that of the supreme sacrifice, is about to strike (see John 13:1; 17:1). But he wishes, once more, to eat the Passover with his disciples (see Luke 22:15). And he is going to institute the new Passover, where the lamb sacrificed will be himself (see I Cor. 5:7; I Peter 1:19; John 1:29; Rev. 5:6, 12-13).

A deep mystery hangs over this last meal: "Truly, I say to you, one of you will betray me" (vs. 21). A great perplexity seizes the disciples. An anguished doubt is revealed in the question, "Is it I, Lord?" The reply of Jesus is not a precise accusation but rather a recollection of the words of Psalm 41:9 (see John 13:18): "Even my bosom friend in whom I trusted, who ate of my bread, has lifted his heel against me."

Jesus knows that in dying he fulfills the destiny of the Son of Man, according to the pre-established plan of God. He is the Suffering Servant announced by the prophet (Isa. 53:3-8). He is the "shepherd of the sheep" who gives his life for his own (Zech. 13:7; compare John 10:11, 17-18). Everything that happens he has foreseen and known, including the treason of Judas. But the guilt of Judas is not attenuated: "It would have been better for that man if he had not been born" (vs. 24; see 18:6-7).

The mystery of Judas does not cease to trouble the Christian. How could one of the Apostles, intermingling each day in the life of Jesus, betray him? Why did Jesus, who reads the heart, choose this man and make him one of the Twelve? (Matt. 10:4). Did such a fate rest upon Judas that he was "destined" to betray? (see John 13:27).

We will never resolve this enigma. But we must place the case of Judas within the whole of the biblical revelation so as not to falsify its meaning. Note first of all that in affirming the responsibility of Judas, Jesus excludes all "fatalism." We are ignorant of the motives of this man. John makes of him a covetous person, a "thief" (12:6), which does not seem to exhaust the depths of his treachery. It is allowable to ask whether Judas was not a Zealot for whom the Messianic Era signified a political revolution. He had waited in vain for Jesus to manifest his power. Perhaps in "delivering" him he desired to force him to manifest himself. This could explain his final remorse (27:3-4).

The Old Testament cites an analogous case of a man chosen by God and afterwards rejected—King Saul. The line between "rebels" and "chosen ones" is not drawn between the Elect People and the pagan nations but through the very midst of Israel and through the very midst of the Church. Indeed, is it not necessary to add, through the very heart of each one of us? Are we not all pardoned "rebels"? The whole Bible reminds us that those who are called to co-operate in the work of salvation are "signs" of the mercy of God, always wholly without merit (see Exod. 33:19), just as the rebels are "signs" of a humanity in revolt against God which, without God's mercy, would utterly perish. The gospel tells us that on the cross Jesus Christ takes on himself the consequences of this rebellion in order to set us free. This is the "good news."

But are not certain ones, by their conscious refusal of God's grace, forever shut out from this mercy, and is not Judas one of these? That remains the secret of God (see 12:31-32). This betrayal by one who belonged to the most intimate circle of followers remains a serious warning for the Church in every age.

The institution of the Lord's Supper is reported not only by the first three Gospels but also by Paul (I Cor. 11:23-26). Jesus returns thanks, breaks the bread, and gives it to his disciples, saying, "Take, eat; this is my body" (some manuscripts of Luke add: "which is given for you. Do this in remembrance of me," Luke 22:19, margin; see I Cor. 11:24). The broken bread is the visible sign of the body of Jesus which is about to be broken on the cross for the salvation of the world. In eating it his disciples become one with him in his death and in his resurrection, members of his Body. Jesus is "the bread of life" which nourishes his people with his own substance and gives them life (see John 6:32, 48, 51, 63).

Afterwards Jesus takes the cup and gives thanks anew. In the Jewish tradition, a giving of thanks preceded each course. Jesus passes the cup to his disciples, saying: "Drink of it, all of you; for this is my blood of the covenant, which is poured out for many for the forgiveness of sins." This saying refers to the institution of the Covenant at Sinai (Exod. 24:6-8; compare Zech. 9:9-11). Moses sprinkled the people with the blood of the victim after having poured out half of it on the altar. This blood, according to the ancient conception, put the people in communion with the altar where the sacrifice was offered. It sealed the Covenant of the people with God. The Apostles drink from the same cup that Jesus drank from, even as they eat the same bread he ate (see I Cor. 10:16-17). By his blood Jesus seals the New Covenant which Jeremiah had proclaimed. This Covenant, of which the Covenant of Sinai was an anticipation, restores their communion with God and also their unity in him. It involves the conversion of the heart. It removes sin (Jer. 31:31-34).

The words spoken by Jesus during this last meal clearly express what was only an implication until then—the redemptive significance of his death. He gives his life for the salvation of his people.

We have seen the figure of the Suffering Servant of Isaiah 53 taking form more and more clearly throughout our study of the Gospel. Jesus is this Servant, unrecognized, rejected, led as a sheep to the slaughter. No one understands, at the moment, the meaning of these sufferings, the meaning of this death, not even the closest disciples. It is said of the Servant that "he poured out his soul to death," that "he bore the sin of many," that he "made intercession for the transgressors." He is the True Israel who bears the sins of the people and atones for them in his own Person. He announces the coming of the Son of Man who alone can effectively take on him the sin of humanity and open the way of life and of liberty, because he alone is innocent.

That is why the celebration of the Passover ends on a note of victory and of joy. Jesus will no more drink of the fruit of the vine in this world, but he will drink it "new" with his people in the Kingdom. This glorious certainty makes of the Lord's Supper a joyous meal. It is a "eucharist," that is to say, a thanksgiving for the salvation won by the sacrifice of Jesus Christ. But it has also an eschatological meaning; that is, it is directed toward the coming of the Lord—it announces the Messianic banquet, the unity of the children of God in the joy of his love and grace.

By what grievous mystery has this meal where Jesus crowns his love, this meal which celebrates his sacrifice and announces his coming, this meal which seals the unity of believers nourished by the same word and the same bread—by what mystery has this meal become a sign of division between Christians? Satan not only set himself up in the heart of Judas and in the midst of the chamber of the Last Supper; he has established himself at the very heart of the sanctuary, tearing Christendom apart, preventing it from being reunited at the same table to announce the victory of the Risen One. The meal of love and of pardon has become the occasion for Christians mutually to exclude one another. The sin of the Pharisees has become ours. We have preferred our forms to the grace of God humbly received. Have not we also, by our divisions and our shortcomings, betrayed our Lord and his holy will?

Each celebration of the Lord's Supper is the joyous announcement of his victory and the sad remembrance of our betrayals, a renewed offering of our lives "as a living sacrifice, holy and acceptable to God" (Rom. 12:1), and the hope of the final fulfillment.

On the Mount of Olives (26:30-46; Mark 14:26-42; Luke 22:39-46)

The hymns which were sung at the close of the Passover meal were Psalms 115-118. Jesus betakes himself to the Garden of Olives, separated from the city by the Brook Kidron. He announces to his disciples—those indeed who had just cele-

brated the Last Supper with him!—that he is going to be for
them, that night, an occasion of falling. He cites the words of
Zechariah 13:7: "I will strike the shepherd, and the sheep of the
flock will be scattered" (Matt. 26:31).

Jesus knows the weakness of the Apostles much better than they
do themselves; he knows that they will forsake him. Once more
he announces to them his resurrection. It is in Galilee, there
where they have worked together, that he makes an appointment
to meet them.

Peter shows himself to be the impulsive one which he has always been. The idea that he could deny his Master scandalizes
him. He is dangerously sure of himself: "Though they all fall
away because of you, I will never fall away." He believes himself to be stronger than his brothers. It will be necessary to
shatter his presumption by the dreadful experience of denial.
Jesus warns him. But Peter does not believe it. He is ready to die
for his Master! "And so said all the disciples." If it had been a
question of fighting for Jesus, without doubt they would have
done that! But it involved something entirely different. Temptation
takes us unawares; it comes under forms for which we are not
prepared. This is why it is the part of wisdom to fear it and to
count on nothing but the sole fidelity of God (compare the petition in the Lord's Prayer, 6:13).

The last hour is come. Jesus awaits his arrest. The place to
which he has withdrawn, Gethsemane—"oil press," calls to mind
the words of the prophet:

> I have trodden the wine press alone,
>   and from the peoples no one was with me;
>
> .   .   .   .
>
> I looked, but there was no one to help;
>   I was appalled, but there was no one to uphold
>   (Isa. 63:3-5).

Jesus is about to descend into the last solitude where no one can
follow him. He takes with him his three most intimate disciples,
Peter, James, and John, and confides his anguish to them: "My
soul is very sorrowful, even to death." He asks them to "watch"
with him—a request unique in the entire Gospel—but even that
will be refused him.

The Gospels show Jesus prostrate, face to the ground, beseech-

ing his Father to spare him "this cup"—the bitter cup of abandonment and death (compare 20:22). But the entreaty concludes
in an act of total submission: "not as I will, but as thou wilt."
Is not the will of the Father his life, his reason for existence?
"Thy will be done" (vs. 42; see 6:10; 12:50; John 6:38; Heb.
10:5-9). But this will *costs* him; it is in this that he is made truly
our brother (Heb. 4:15; 5:8-9).

Jesus three times entreats his Father. Three times he arises
and finds his disciples sleeping. Peter—this Peter so sure of
himself—has not been able to watch one hour with his Master.
And Jesus warns the Apostles once more: "The spirit indeed is
willing, but the flesh is weak." In biblical language the "flesh"
designates human nature in all its weakness and fallibility. It
is opposed to the spirit, which comes from God and draws us toward him. Paul has characterized the struggle which sets man at
war with himself: "I do not do the good I want, but the evil I
do not want is what I do" (Rom. 7:18-20; 8:5-6). Temptation is
going to find the disciples tragically disarmed since they have not
had the strength to watch one hour with their Master. Who are
the "sinners" into whose hands the Son of Man is betrayed? (vs.
45). An Apostle, the leaders of Israel, a Roman magistrate—the
religious authorities and the secular authorities, the "qualified"
representatives of a humanity which does not want God.

Some people are astonished that the prospect of death should
have thrown Jesus into such an agony. The objection is not new.
Socrates, dying stoically without uttering a complaint, has been
contrasted with him. Why did Jesus' spirit recoil at the last minute
before a death which he had foreseen and announced? Is Jesus in
his turn unsettled by the scandal of the Cross which disturbed
the disciples?

No one could without rashness seek to penetrate the mystery
of the agony of the Son of God. Jesus has let us know his anguish,
but not what passed between him and his Father at this hour. Let
us recall simply that in the biblical revelation death is not something "natural," something "normal." Life is natural and normal,
for God is the God of life, and death is the negation of him. According to a word of the Book of Job, death is "the king of
terrors" (Job 18:14). The Bible does not proclaim the immor-
tality of the soul as a property which belongs to it by nature. It
proclaims the miracle of the Resurrection. John shows Jesus
deeply agitated at the tomb of Lazarus (John 11:33, 38). He

measures, as no mortal man can, the horror of this break, this "end" which is death.

In the second place, let us understand what sort of death is involved for Jesus. God has come to his people in the Person of his Anointed, and his people respond to him with a deicide; they kill the "heir" (21:38). The acme of love is about to produce the acme of hate. The coming of the Son causes men to commit the worst crime they have ever committed. God "delivers" him "into the hands of sinners."

Let us be thankful to the evangelists for having reported to us this struggle. The one whom God has given us as Savior is not a Stoic, nor a god whose humanity was only specious. No, he is one who cried out to God with tears (see Heb. 5:7), and begged him to spare him. This is why he is able to sympathize with our griefs, carry our sorrows, and give us the strength to pray, in our hours of greatest confusion and abandonment, "Not as I will, but as thou wilt."

Let us be thankful also for the honesty with which the Apostles have confessed their own failures. They have preserved and transmitted the memory of this dreadful night when they could not watch one hour with their Master—and afterwards abandoned him. They tell us this for our warning. Pascal has reminded us that Jesus is in agony until the end of the world, and we should not sleep during this entire time. Pascal understands that the combat of the Lord against the powers of evil and death continues to the end of time, "until he has put all his enemies under his feet" (I Cor. 15:25-26). Is the Church watching with him? Or are our eyes "heavy"?

The Arrest (26:47-56)

A "great crowd" draws near, made up doubtless of the Temple guard, which is armed, besides slaves or mercenaries furnished with clubs. What a deployment of forces to arrest a man who does not dream of resisting! Judas salutes his Master and kisses him, which is the sign agreed upon. The response of Jesus, "Friend, why are you here?" may mean either, "Why have you come to this place?" or "Why do you kiss me?" This remark is sad, not harsh. It does not close the possibility of repentance to Judas.

How great is the temptation to defend Jesus with arms! There is no doubt that the Apostles would gladly have died in such a defense. But a more difficult sort of courage is demanded of them—

the courage which the Sermon on the Mount requires. The saying, "All who take the sword will perish by the sword," is likely a maxim; in any case, it is a fact. Murder calls out murder; war invites war. This is the plane of human vengeance, or at best, the law of retaliation. But the Kingdom which Jesus inaugurated is of another order: to defend him by violence is to betray him. Would that the Church had always remembered this, and that it had never put the sword at the service of the cause of God!

Verse 53, which Matthew alone reports, emphasizes the sovereign liberty of Jesus. Had he wished, he could even at that hour have implored his Father, who would have dispatched to him "twelve legions of angels." It is God, and not man, who controls his destiny. The Scriptures are being fulfilled (vs. 54). Everything unfolds as the prophets had announced, right up to this cowardly nocturnal enterprise against a man who spoke daily in the Temple in the sight and to the knowledge of all without being hindered (vss. 55-56).

The disciples lose heart and flee.

An Examination and a Denial (26:57-75)

The two stories of the examination of Jesus before the Sanhedrin and the denial of Peter in the court of the high priest follow each other; there is no doubt that the contrast is intended. At the very hour when Jesus is openly confessing his Messiahship before men, his disciple denies knowing him.

The Sanhedrin has to be brought together hastily in the middle of the night. The trial preserves, outwardly at least, the accepted legal forms. The presence of two or three witnesses is required (Deut. 17:6). The saying regarding the destruction of the Temple is the first valid charge, for it has a Messianic significance: the Messiah was to renew all things and construct a new Temple. By testifying that Jesus said, "I am able to destroy . . . ," the witnesses twist Jesus' words (see 24:2; see also John 2:19-22). Jesus remains silent. Then the high priest decides on a direct attack: "I adjure you by the living God, tell us if you are the Christ, the Son of God."

It is sometimes asked whether the "You have said so" of Jesus was an affirmative reply. What follows immediately thereafter permits no doubt. It refers to Daniel 7:13—the vision of the Son of Man coming on the clouds from heaven—and to Psalm 110:1. Both of these passages are regarded as Messianic. It is at the hour when he is going to die that Jesus, for the first time, publicly affirms his royalty (see 16:16-17, 20). He knows that this confession is his undoing.

One who heard a blasphemy was supposed to tear his garments. The high priest officially accuses Jesus of blasphemy and the condemnation to death is pronounced. Jesus is taunted with mocking and spitting. Since he is a prophet, let him divine who has struck him! In this, prophecy was fulfilled (Isa. 50:5-6).

Peter is in the court, anxious no doubt over the fate of his Master, eager for news. A servant recognizes him. "You also were with Jesus the Galilean." To be with Jesus—was not that yesterday still his privilege and his pride? "Even if I must die with you, I will not deny you" (26:35). And now, the question of a servant is sufficient to make him respond, "I do not know what you mean." This is the first step toward total denial, leading to a second where he says with an oath, "I do not know the man," and a third in which he invokes a "curse" on himself and swears, "I do not know the man."

Do not judge Peter too quickly. Do not we, in the course of petty conversations or in an ironic or hostile group, slip into subtle denials? It is probably not danger which provokes Peter's denial; it is more likely his confusion, and the tone of the maid, and the fact that his accent makes him stand out.

But such explanations in the last analysis explain nothing. Anything can make us fall when God withdraws his hand. Simon Peter must learn that, given over to himself, he can do nothing. That alone could heal him of his presumption. The saying of Jesus about his denial comes back to Peter; he weeps. When he later meets the Risen One he will for the first time know what *grace* is.

Deliberation of the Chief Priests and the Death of Judas (27:1-10)

The chief priests and the elders hold council. The problem is, how to secure the death of Jesus. The Sanhedrin had jurisdiction over Israelites in everything which concerned the Law (see John 18:31); it could put a guilty person to death. The customary method was by stoning (see Acts 7:57-58). But in this case the Sanhedrin would have exposed itself to the anger of the crowds. Moreover, the problem involved destroying the prestige of Jesus and the movement which his authority had stirred up. To declare that he had proclaimed himself King of the Jews would justify the intervention of Roman authority (see Luke 23:1-2). The Romans would punish him as an insurgent, and inflict on him the torment reserved for slaves—crucifixion. All Jews would then be obliged to acknowledge that the curse of God rested on him: "Cursed be every one who hangs on a tree" (Gal. 3:13; see Deut. 21:22-23).

Without doubt, such was the reasoning which the chief priests used to deliver Jesus to the Roman procurator. But for the evangelist that also is foretold (see 20:19); that also is included in God's plan of salvation. All, both Jews and Gentiles, conspire to put to death the Son of God.

The condemnation of Jesus upsets Judas. This seems indeed to indicate that he had believed that there would be either an acquittal or a manifestation of power by the Messiah (see comment on 26:20-25). Had Judas desired to force the hand of God? He returns the money to the priests (see Matt. 27:3). He shouts to them the innocence of his Master and draws this atrociously cynical word in reply: "What is that to us? See to it yourself." The remorse of Judas is outside of the presence of God; his end reveals this, for his remorse does not lead him to repentance but to despair. Judas takes his own life. Thus Matthew shows us that he who rejects proffered grace destroys himself.

Jesus Before Pilate (27:11-31)

Pontius Pilate was governor ("procurator" is the exact term) of Judea from A.D. 26 to A.D. 36. His name remains forever attached to the confession of the Christian faith; "suffered under Pontius Pilate," the Apostles' Creed has it, indicating the historic facts—the time and the place—of Jesus' death (see Luke 3:1; Acts 3:13).

The indictment which the ecclesiastical authorities pronounced against Jesus comes out again in the question of Pilate: "Are you the King of the Jews?" The reply of Jesus could signify, "It is you who say it"; it seems, however, to be rather an affirmation (see 26:64). Immediately his adversaries overwhelm him with accusations, but he disdains to reply to their calumnies (see 26: 63). The Gospels by Mark and Matthew both lay stress on the silence of Jesus. In him is fulfilled to the very end the destiny of the Suffering Servant of Isaiah:

He was oppressed, and he was afflicted,
    yet he opened not his mouth;

> like a lamb that is led to the slaughter,
> and like a sheep that before its shearers is dumb,
> so he opened not his mouth (Isa. 53:7).

But there was such a dignity, such a grandeur, in his silence that Pilate was impressed by it (vs. 14; see also vs. 18).

It happened that the people could obtain by acclamation the pardon of a prisoner. This does not seem to have been a regular custom. Pilate, with the intention of saving Jesus, offered to the assembled crowd the deliverance of a prisoner, and gave them the choice between Jesus and Barabbas. This latter name is not complete, for it means "son of Abbas." According to an ancient manuscript, the name was "Jesus, son of Abbas" (vs. 16, see margin). The choice, then, would be between Jesus son of Abbas and Jesus the Messiah. Barabbas is a man condemned for sedition and murder (see Mark 15:7; Luke 23:19).

Matthew inserts here an episode which he alone reports and which, in his thought, accentuates the responsibility of Pilate— the intervention of Pilate's wife, warned in a dream of the crime which is about to be perpetrated: "Have nothing to do with that righteous man." It is a pagan who proclaims the Messiah of Israel "righteous"!

The chief priests instigate the crowd to demand not Jesus, but Barabbas (vs. 20). We grasp here, in a very lifelike way, the demonism of an insidiously underhanded propaganda—the crowd clamors for that for which they have been made to clamor. Are these the same people who, one week earlier, acclaimed Jesus and cried, "Hosanna to the Son of David!" (21:9), people to whom Jesus has never done anything but good? Where are his Galilean friends hiding, far from the judgment hall where one of their number is condemned? Among the thousands of pilgrims gathered at Jerusalem during these days it should have been easy to stir up a crowd. Is it not of these poor crowds that Jesus is thinking when he prays, "Father, forgive them; for they know not what they do"? (Luke 23:34).

Pilate does not have this excuse. He knows that he is going to condemn an innocent man. But state policy outweighs the law. Tumult increases. The peace of Jerusalem is worth more than the life of one man! Pilate "washed his hands" of this murder. He seems to have borrowed for the occasion a Jewish custom in order to clear himself before the people of the crime in which he acquiesced (see Deut. 21:6-9; Pss. 26:6; 73:13). He does not even have the courage to assume the responsibility for his acts. Thus the abdication of secular authority leaves the way free for the passions of men.

The people are ready with a terrible remark: "His blood be on us and on our children!" Matthew alone has dared to preserve this saying. Addressing himself to people of Jewish origin, he lays bare the responsibility of Israel. This responsibility will be emphasized by the Apostles, not to exonerate the Roman authority but to remind the Elect People that it is they themselves who have rejected their Messiah and to incite them to repentance and faith (see Acts 2:36; 3:12-18). Throughout the history of the Church, men have often played on this culpability in order to persecute the Jewish people. Anti-Semitism is an accursed fruit of Christian self-righteousness which at this point overtakes the Pharisaism condemned by Jesus. Men forget that "salvation is from the Jews" (John 4:22), and that Jesus and his Apostles were Jews. They forget above all that these Jews who condemned Jesus, this Pilate who delivered him to them, these soldiers who insulted him, represent rebellious humanity, arrayed against God—that humanity which is also ours. "For God has consigned all men to disobedience, that he may have mercy upon all" (Rom. 11:32).

Those condemned to crucifixion were first beaten with rods (vs. 26). The soldiers added derision to the suffering (vss. 27-31). The scarlet robe was likely that of a Roman officer. The reed symbolized a royal scepter. This masquerade, aimed beyond Jesus, strikes at the Jewish people, ridiculing their faith in a King-Messiah. To the cruelty was added mockery and spitting. Human sadism, once unleashed, gives itself free course.

The Crucifixion (27:32-56)

Custom demanded that the condemned should carry his own cross to the place of execution. If he were too weak, the soldiers commandeered a passer-by. No disciple is there to relieve his Master staggering under the load. The Gospels have preserved the name of the man who rendered this last service to Jesus— Simon of Cyrene. Doubtless he witnessed the Crucifixion. Mark describes him as the father of Alexander and Rufus, showing that these two last were well known in the Church (Mark 15:21; see Rom. 16:13).

The story of the Crucifixion is one of remarkable restraint. It refrains from trying to describe the agony of Jesus. But it indicates in some brief touches the indifference, the cynicism, and the irony of those who watched him die.

The soldiers give him wine "mingled with gall" (vs. 34). There is perhaps in this a reminiscence of Psalm 69 (see vs. 21). Dying criminals were given a bitter drink for the purpose of assuaging their pain. Jesus refuses it. He will retain a clear consciousness to the very end. They strip the clothes from the condemned, nail him to the cross, and then raise the cross upright. The soldiers are indifferent to the torture they inflict. They draw lots for his clothing and seat themselves to keep guard over him.

The ground of the condemnation is written over the cross: "This is Jesus the King of the Jews." The purpose of this inscription is to ridicule Jewish messianism. But in the eyes of Christians, Rome, without intending it, proclaimed the truth. This executed criminal is the King who will come again in power and glory. The prophecy of Isaiah 53 is fulfilled. Both in his life and in his death Jesus is the foretold Servant.

They crucified along with Jesus two "robbers," who may have been rebels (or Zealots) who wished to make the Messianic cause triumph at the point of the sword. Passers-by derided him. They cited the words of Jesus about the Temple (vs. 40; see John 2:19) and mocked his weakness. Truly, what a strange "Son of God"! "Save yourself!"

In the story of the Temptation (4:1-11) and at several other places in the course of the Gospel, Matthew has indicated that it is precisely in not seeking to "save himself" that Jesus shows himself to be the authentic Son of God. Once more the contrast is manifest between the thoughts of men and the thoughts of God (see 16:23). Once more Satan tempts Jesus: "Let him come down now from the cross, and we will believe in him." It is the ecclesiastical authorities who thus mock, and in so doing they deny the most profound revelation given to Israel—the necessity for the agony of the Righteous One. One single voice in the course of the trial styled Jesus "righteous," the voice of a pagan (vs. 19).

These contrasts are deliberate. The Gospel by Matthew joins in the task in which Paul is engrossed (see Rom. chs. 9-11), to summon their Jewish brothers to repentance by cutting off all retreat, convincing them of their guilt, and showing them from the Scriptures that everything was foreseen and foretold (hence the reference to Pss. 69, 22, and Isa. 53). They must be incited to jealousy by being shown that the pagans have discerned, through a direct revelation of God, what they themselves in their blindness have rejected and scorned (vss. 19, 54).

From the sixth hour (noon) until the ninth, darkness covered the land (vs. 45). This is the hour of judgment, the darkness of the silence of God, the darkness of his absence! It is expressed in that terrible cry which only Mark and Matthew have been bold enough to reproduce: "My God, my God, why hast thou forsaken me?" These words open Psalm 22, which concludes in a hymn of victory. But this victory will be seen only at the Resurrection. For the evangelists, this hour is indeed the hour of darkness, and there is no reason to attenuate its significance. It is the hour when the One who consents to be the Servant, the humiliated Servant, drinks to the dregs the cup of human sin (see Isa. 53:3-9 and Phil. 2:5-9).

One of the onlookers, in a gesture of pity, holds up to the crucified a sponge filled with vinegar. The others mock. Misunderstanding the words spoken by Jesus, they conclude that he is calling Elijah to his aid. They see in this cry the supreme admission of weakness on the part of this messianic pretender.

After a last great cry (see Heb. 5:7), Jesus "yielded up his spirit." Luke likely makes explicit what is implied in this saying of Matthew when he reports Jesus' words, "Father, into thy hands I commit my spirit!" (Luke 23:46; see Ps. 31:5). This death is not a defeat but a final victory. This stands out clearly from what follows (vss. 51-54).

The veil of the Temple is torn (vs. 51; see Mark 15:38). This veil shut in the Holy of Holies from profane eyes. Only the high priest could enter it. The rending marks the end of the old worship, an end which Jesus had foretold (24:2; see also 21:12-13). The Gospel does not explain the meaning of this symbolic event. Every Jew, however, would understand it as a judgment of God. All Christians should see in it what the Letter to the Hebrews indicates—access into the sanctuary is henceforth opened by Jesus Christ to all believers; and, perhaps it should be added, the ancient notion which opposes the "sacred" to the "profane" is abolished (see Heb. 9:1-14; 10:19-22). The hour has come to worship "in spirit and truth" (John 4:23-24).

Verses 51-54 express the cosmic significance of the death and resurrection of Jesus Christ. The "signs" given in this passage are signs that usher in the end of the world in the final resurrection. What Matthew desires to signify by these miracles is the import of the event which has just taken place. The earth trembles on its foundations, for this is the hour of God's judgment. One world is disappearing, another is being born.

The Roman centurion and those who with him have watched the execution are the first to confess Jesus as Son of God. According to Matthew, it is the phenomena which accompany Jesus' death which impress these soldiers. According to Mark, it is rather the extraordinary character of Jesus' agony which provokes the centurion's confession of faith (Mark 15:39; see also margin). Whatever it was, this confession constitutes the first fruits of a future harvest; it foretells the conversion of the "nations" (see 28:19).

The Crucifixion has still other witnesses. Some women, Matthew tells us, have witnessed the agony of their Lord "from afar." They had accompanied him from Galilee to Jerusalem to "provide" for him out of their means (see Luke 8:2-3). Nothing is told us of them and their grief, save that they are there. All the Gospels testify of the attitude of Jesus toward women, of the kindness with which he treated them. He gave them their human dignity. He revealed to them the grace of pardon. He provoked in them a gratitude and a love which were unflagging. Prior to Jesus, women were regarded as inferior beings, religiously speaking. The Apostolic Church came to know thereafter that all, both men and women, are the objects of the same grace and the same salvation (see Gal. 3:27-38).

The Burial (27:57-66)

Joseph of Arimathea is mentioned for the first time. Matthew specifies that he was "a rich man." Perhaps he has in mind the prophecy of Isaiah, "And they made his grave . . . with a rich man in his death" (Isa. 53:9). Has he not in detail shown Jesus fulfilling in his Person the destiny of the Suffering Servant? It is a strange thing that it is neither the Apostles nor near relatives who render this last service of love to Jesus. Doubtless they were unable to do it. Only two women, of whom one was Mary Magdalene, witnessed the burial.

We have already seen the manner in which our Gospel contrasts light and shadow. Between the gesture of love by Joseph of Arimathea and the news of the Resurrection the author inserts the proceedings of the high priests and Pharisees. Their hatred is not appeased. They suspect the disciples of plotting a deception. Pilate grants them the guard which they request, but he leaves the responsibility of it to them.

The Resurrection (28:1-20)

The Empty Tomb
(28:1-15; Mark 16:1-8; Luke 24:1-10; John 20:1-18)

The women have respected the Sabbath rest. But at dawn they set out. Matthew does not say, as do Mark and Luke, that they come to embalm the body. They know indeed that they cannot do it (see 27:66). And has Jesus not been embalmed beforehand? (26:12). They come just to be there, as we also go to the tomb of a beloved person. Then, too, do they perhaps hope for the miracle which the chief priests fear? Had not Jesus foretold his resurrection?

"And behold, there was a great earthquake" (vs. 2; see 27:51-54). To the darkness of judgment succeeds the resplendent light of the Resurrection, the descent of an angel. The guards become "like dead men," terrified by the heavenly vision. But to the women who have believed, the angel says, "Do not be afraid; for I know that you seek Jesus." God turns his face of mercy toward those who seek him (see Luke 1:30; 5:10; Rev. 1:17-18).

Jesus grants to these humble women whom he has healed and saved, and who love him with a great love, the grace of being messengers of the Resurrection. The angel commands them to go find the disciples. Jesus will meet them in Galilee. The women run toward the city, full of *fear* and of *joy*. How could they not fear a God so powerful? How could they not tremble for joy? Their Master, the crucified of yesterday, is living!

And behold, a new favor. Jesus himself comes to meet them and salutes them, doubtless with the classic Hebrew salutation of "Peace" (see Luke 24:36, margin). Then "they came up and took hold of his feet and worshiped him" (vs. 9; see 28:17). This term "worshiped" points to the supervening change—the Master they venerate is become "the Lord," the One whom they adore as God himself, the One before whom they prostrate themselves.

Ah, certainly, the stories of the Resurrection are full of mystery. None of the Gospels tells us "how" it happened. The story

of the angelic appearances, the record of the appearances of Jesus
himself, the place of these appearances (Galilee, Jerusalem),
differ from one Gospel to another. Three elements, nevertheless,
are common to all four Gospels—the empty tomb, the announcement of the Resurrection to the women, and the meeting of the
disciples with the Risen One. The tradition preserved by Matthew
accentuates, as it has already done in connection with the death
of Jesus, the objective character of the event—the earthquake,
the testimony of the guards, their fright. What he wishes to em-
phasize is that we are not dealing here with "visions," which
could be purely subjective, but rather with a sovereign intervention of God.

But the intervention of God is ever recognized as such solely
by faith. Matthew sets over against the humble and adoring faith
of the women the unbelief of the chief priests (vss. 11-15). To
the very end they remain closed against all evidence. They bribe
the guards to circulate the report that the body of Jesus had been
carried off by Jesus' own disciples (vss. 11-15). The evangelist
concludes: "This story has been spread among the Jews to this
day." We certainly have here the echo of a very ancient controversy between Jews and Christians on the subject of the empty
tomb. This controversy explains why Matthew believed it necessary to recount (he alone does it) the two episodes in 27:62-66
and 28:11-15.

The Commission Given to the Disciples (28:16-20)

We have seen that a "mountain" is, in the Old Testament, one
of the privileged places of divine revelation (Exod. 19:3; I Kings
19:8). It was "on the mountain" that Jesus promulgated the law
of the Kingdom (Matt. 5:1), it was on "a high mountain" that
he was transfigured before his disciples (Matt. 17:1). And it is
once more on "the mountain" that the Risen One meets the
Apostles (vs. 16). "And when they saw him they worshiped
him" (vs. 17; see 28:9). That is to say, they recognized him as
the Son of God. Nevertheless, the Gospel tells us, some had
doubts. We see once more in this feature the mystery of the appearances of the Risen One. They did not recognize him at first
but only when he made himself known. The evidence is in the
category of faith (see Luke 24:11, 25, 37; John 20:15-16, 24-
29). Doubt remains possible. Unbelief is not the monopoly of
the Jewish authorities who crucified the Lord; it has spread even

to the disciples. Let us be thankful for the apostolic tradition which did not hesitate to confess the human weakness of the disciples to whom Jesus is about to give a commission to evangelize the world! It is indeed by his power alone that they will go everywhere he will command them to go.

And it is this power which the Risen One declares. He speaks as sovereign Lord of heaven and earth. To the freely accepted humiliation of the Servant succeeds his elevation to royalty (see Isa. 52:13-15; 53:12). He is no longer only the "King of the Jews" (see Matt. 2:2; 21:4-5; 27:37) but is the King of the nations (see Isa. 49:5-6; Matt. 25:31-32). His words recall the prophecy of Daniel about the enthronement of the Son of Man:

> And to him was given dominion
>   and glory and kingdom,
> that all peoples, nations, and languages
>   should serve him;
> his dominion is an everlasting dominion,
>   which shall not pass away,
> and his kingdom one
>   that shall not be destroyed
>   (Dan. 7:14; see Phil. 2:8-11).

The evangelization of the nations (that is to say, of the Gentiles) in the last times was an idea found in Jewish eschatological writings as well as in the Old Testament. We have seen that according to Matthew the priority granted to Israel was a priority in time only. The faith of the centurion (8:10-11; see also another centurion in 27:54) and that of the Canaanite woman (15:22) had already forecast the day when the good news would be proclaimed to the Gentiles. Jesus testified that he had done everything possible to bring the people of the Covenant back to God (23:37-39). With the Resurrection and the Ascension and the descent of the Holy Spirit we enter into "the last times." The hour of the nations has struck. It is to them that the good news must now be proclaimed (see 24:14).

Jesus confronts his disciples, and through them the Church in every age, with a mission which extends to the ends of the earth. It is the Mighty One who speaks, the One who has conquered sin and death. As he has taught his disciples—and the Gospel by Matthew never ceases to lay stress on this teaching—so they, in their turn, are commissioned to teach. Baptism will be the seal of God put on this teaching. Here again stress is laid on putting into practice the word which has been heard. We have seen how the necessity of *doing the will of God* runs like a scarlet thread through all the instructions of Jesus.

The trinitarian baptismal formula, "in the name of the Father and of the Son and of the Holy Spirit," is found only this once in the entire New Testament. It is affirmed in all the great Christian confessions. The baptism of John introduced at the beginning of the Gospel, which Jesus received (3:6, 13), was a baptism of repentance for the forgiveness of sins. In the Acts we see the Apostles baptizing "in the name of Jesus Christ," and this baptism is "for the forgiveness of your sins" (Acts 2:38-39). What is the significance of the formula "in the name of Jesus Christ"? It is into his death that we Christians are baptized. This means that we die to our old life and are born into a new life in communion with the Risen One (see Rom. 6:3-4). It is this union of Jesus with us and of us with Jesus which constitutes the radical newness of Christian baptism. But the change of heart which Jesus works in us is accompanied by the gift of the Spirit (Acts 2:38; see 10:44-48). And all that is the work of the Father who has raised Jesus and given the Holy Spirit, the Father who calls us to believe in his Son (see Acts 2:32-33, 36). Thus, in this new birth which baptism signifies, the Father, the Son, and the Holy Spirit are all three present and active. The preaching of the Apostles will be the joyous news of the love of God manifested in Jesus Christ. And those who believe this news will receive the seal of baptism, the sign of their passing from death to life.

Jesus concludes the commission given to his Church with a promise. And what a promise! "Lo, I am with you always, to the close of the age."

To these men who in a cowardly manner had abandoned him in the supreme trial, to these men who still perhaps doubt, Jesus makes no reproach. He charges them to pursue his work, to proclaim his salvation. He assures them of his fidelity to them.

He will be present in their midst (see 18:20) through the Word and the sacraments, and through the Holy Spirit—invisibly present everywhere and always—*to the close of the age;* that is to say, to that day when the Lord of glory will reveal himself to all eyes as the victorious King of a new creation.